HEAVEN
IN SIGHT

PETER JACKSON
WITH
HELENA ROGERS

AMBASSADOR
Belfast Northern Ireland Greenville South Carolina

Heaven in Sight
© 1999

ISBN 1 84030 052 3

Ambassador Publications
a division of
Ambassador Productions Ltd.
Providence House
16 Hillview Avenue,
Belfast, BT5 6JR
Northern Ireland

Emerald House
1 Chick Springs Road, Suite 203
Greenville,
South Carolina 29609, USA
www.emeraldhouse.com

LIST OF CONTENTS

CHAPTER ONE
HEAVEN IN SIGHT

THE OLD PIANO STOOD against the living room wall. It was our most valuable possession, although it's better days had been seen a long time ago. In paying for it my parents enabled the people over the road to keep their home. We knew this because we discovered a letter amongst the dusty strings which revealed that unless the rent was paid, the family would be evicted.

But to me it represented more than a rent payment. It stood as the priceless key to the future - an opening to the wonderful world of music and a bottom rung on the ladder of my destiny.

In fact I didn't spend as much time with my piano as I would have liked. My home had become a place I went to only during the holidays. The rest of my time was spent in residential schools for the blind where I had been sent from the age of two after losing my sight through measles.

I found it desperately hard at first - I could not understand the desperation of my mother with four young children and another on the way - all I knew was that I had been abandoned in a world of darkness.

In those first few years at 'The Sunshine Homes for Blind Babies', I rarely saw my mother or my family, but as I got older and went on to the Birmingham Royal Institute for the Blind, I was allowed home for the holidays.

By this time, however, my family had become fragile memories which could never fully be restored to their natural homely intimacies. I continually came and went to the spartan, impersonal regime of training school while my brothers and sisters remained comfortably at home, so I could never be a fully integrated part of the family group. I felt the presumed rejection very deeply.

I never stopped wanting to be part of the family, however, and school could only be borne because at the end of each term, I could go home for the holidays.

My parents made an enormous sacrifice to buy me the piano - especially as they knew it would only be used for about ten weeks of the year. But as soon as it became obvious that their little blind boy was not so much a helpless tragic loss as a burgeoning new talent, they determined to encourage this sudden up-turn in their fortunes and sink all in the purchase of the prized piano.

Emotion overcame me when it stood, at last, proudly and over-poweringly against the wall of the living room. My brother and sisters watched in awe as I seated myself on a chair (finances couldn't extend to a piano stool) and began to try out the first pieces I had learned that term. The sounds which filled the crowded living room were cracked and discordant even though I easily played the right notes, but the aged piano had been bought for me - just me - and my heart nearly burst with the wonderful feeling of reconciliation which it represented.

Music fascinated me ever since I could remember, but my ambition was irrevocably decided at the first sound of the notes produced by my teacher on the piano in the school hall. I had never heard anything so wonderful, and I resolved to play like her at my first opportunity. I became somewhat disillusioned when I discovered that it would take me more than just one lesson to produce similar sounds, but after the initial shock, I soon accepted the situation and piano lessons became a real joy.

An additional firing to my ambition came about on hearing the piano tuner at work. If I could, I would station myself beside him in the hall and listen to the delicate changes he made to each string. I would even opt to miss my dinner rather than miss the fascinating interlude.

I listened to the discordant twang, twang, twang as the tuner hit each note, changing the tension of the strings with the tuning key, and I concentrated as the twang gradually mellowed into the resonant dong of pure sound when the tuner had regulated the strings to his satisfaction. I found myself willing him to keep going until I recognised the true level, and would be strangely disappointed if a tuner left a string which to my ears, sounded short of its proper pitch.

Once, on one of my holiday visits home, Mr. Lambert, the piano tuner arrived to attend to my piano. Piano tuning rarely found its way to the top of the list of necessary expenses in our house, so most of the time I contented myself with a sound which jarred on my acute hearing. I did not complain, however, for this was my piano - not anyone else's - and I had sole use of it. I would rather have an out-of-tune piano than no piano at all.

But when Mr. Lambert came, I was enthralled. He would have to work harder on my piano than those at school, because the school ones were regularly tuned and so only needed slight maintenance. I knew mine to be way off pitch, and so it would therefore take much longer. I settled down to listen.

Mr. Lambert waited for me to get bored, but as I remained, fascinated, he turned to me. Putting a lever in my hand, he showed me how to use it, guiding my hand and letting me hear how it altered the sound of the strings. I responded eagerly, and carefully stretched the string to its correct pitch.

"My goodness!" he said, amazed, "if you're not a piano tuner when you grow up, I shall eat my hat!" I glowed with pride and determined that he would never have cause to become hatless.

He came to tune my piano again when I was eleven years old. This time, either he had been in a hurry or perhaps his hearing failed him temporarily, because after he left, the result did not please me at all.

"Mum, he's left the treble sharp," I complained. My mystified mother frowned.

"What do you mean?" she asked, "it sounds fine to me."

"But Mum, it's ever so sharp, listen -" and I demonstrated what I meant.

She remained none the wiser, but after I had insisted that the treble did, indeed, sound sharp, and that with my now highly sensitive ears, I could not cope with it in that condition, she agreed to send for the tuner once more.

"What's the problem?" he asked, good naturedly, when he returned later.

"You've left it a bit too sharp at the top," I explained, reinforcing my claim with a couple of firm chords.

"You're right," he said, thoughtfully, and proceeded to rectify the matter. I listened carefully as he set to work again.

When he had finished he turned to me. "How's that?" he asked.

"Fine," I said with a grin.

"I shall have to be a bit more careful when I come to your house next time, won't I?" he admitted, picking up his tool case.

It always puzzled me when tuners left a piano in a less than perfect condition. To me, the job was so easy. I could clearly define the minute changes in each string, and it jarred on me to hear any left short of their correct pitch. When I eventually went to piano tuning college, therefore, I sailed comparatively smoothly through the course, completing it in three years instead of four. I felt I had been born to the job.

College became the place where I really started to learn. I did not relate to primary school very well. My only interests had been in music, reading, and Braille writing. Lessons in differentiating between coins were fun too - we used to play shops and give the right change, feeling the milled edges of the shillings and the little sixpences; and we also loved rolling the twelve-sided threepenny bits across the desks - they made a lovely 'brrrrrrrrrrr' sound! All the other lessons seemed somewhat pointless to me, and I could not put much effort into them. Only in later years did I come to some understanding as to my ambivalence toward lessons. It seemed to me that we had not been taught the right things. It was all very well to be taught Geography and History, but they did not set blind children up to look after themselves in the world. A knowledge of the rivers of Europe did not help us to change a tap washer or fix a fuse.

It was understandable that we could only learn to read through Braille, but how useful it would have been if we had been taught to write a signature with an ordinary pen. As it turned out, the blind of my generation would leave school unable to sign a cheque or write their names on an official form. We were left dependent on others when we could have been trained to be far more self-sufficient.

Gaps in our education existed even at college. We were taught something called 'Economics', in which we learned about Rates and their collection, and about such things as government grants and government spending, but they did not teach us about mortgages and how to secure our own accommodation. It was not conducive to the independence of the blind person.

My interest could not even be stirred by the compulsory choir practices. A male voice and a mixed voice choir had been formed, plus a voluntary 'Choral Union', and, admittedly, we were introduced to some excellent music. I enjoyed this part of it as I sang Handel's 'Messiah', Coleridge's 'Hiawatha's Wedding Feast' and Armstrong Gibbs 'The Highwayman'.

But there was a 'down' side. For some reason we did not have Braille copies of the parts. A full copy existed, of course, but we were not given individual copies. This meant copying them out in full - in Braille, of course - by hand. It involved us in a lot of painstaking work, especially if we happened to be singing something like 'Worthy the Lamb' or 'The Hallelujah Chorus'. These were essentially fugal - each part singing the same themes but interweaving one after another - and they consisted of hundreds of demi-semi-quaver very quick notes, all of which had to be written one by one. It took hours!

In one area of college life, however - apart from the piano tuning - I could be entirely enthusiastic. The Christian Fellowship took up a lot of my time and I was extremely keen to spread the Gospel. I began college with no interest in Christianity at all, but one of the other students, John, happened to be a superb pianist who played for the Christian Fellowship, so I had to go there to hear him play! He became a good friend, and I respected his opinion although I was far from convinced about Christianity myself.

However, before long I became interested enough to go and hear an American child evangelist who had come to England for a crusade. This proved to be the turning point for me, and following the meeting, I shut myself away in my room - having missed both lunch and tea - and thought the whole thing through. I came out of that room committed to Christ and determined that others should find Him too.

I became very keen indeed - some would say 'nuisance' described me more accurately! I remember somebody saying to me, 'Christianity is like medicine; if you give a dose now and again it will be all right; if you give all the medicine at once, it will kill 'em!' In later years I learned a little more wisdom, but the young are less discerning and one can only leave it to the Lord to keep His hand on the situation.

One way in which our keenness showed itself was in our early morning prayer meetings. We spent an hour or so in prayer before breakfast, when we learned to intercede for people, burdened by the need to bring them to a knowledge of the salvation of God. They were great times, and we saw many come to faith in direct answer to our prayers. But while we prayed, we often forgot the time and committed the unpardonable sin in the college view - we came down late for breakfast!

The staff maintained that if you were late for breakfast, then you had therefore got up late. This did not happen to be true in our case, of course, and it caused something of a dilemma. When we arrived late for breakfast one morning, the supervisor was confused.

"I should punish you for being late," he pointed out severely. "You are quite aware how important it is to be disciplined enough to get up in time. But I realise that in your case you were up in time and that your meeting was the reason for your lateness. All I can say therefore, is that you must not be late again. This must not be an excuse for persistent lateness." From this we learned that one has to be wise, no matter how justifiable the cause.

This reminds me of a story I heard about a student at a Bible college, who did not find it at all easy to get up early in the mornings for the prayer meetings. The other students would not let this sort of thing go on, and used to take it upon themselves to 'encourage' the deeper sleepers to wake up. However, this particular student appeared to be a very keen Christian later in the day, but he had a severe problem with mornings.

His condition was not helped by the method used by the others to rouse him. They would begin by prodding him, and when that produced no effect, they would go on to rock him roughly and bounce him up and down until they got a response! Having achieved their aim, they would then accept that he simply could not be approached much before lunch time, and they ignored his irritability.

But some of the lads did not consider this good enough. They frequently pointed out in no uncertain terms that a Christian should not behave in this way even in he did happen to be woken up from a deep sleep at the crack of dawn. They freely quoted verses like Colossians chapter three, verses nine and ten where it says, 'put off the old man with his deeds.........put on the new man which is renewed..........'

When approached with these worthy comments after lunch, the young man seemed responsive and contrite, and he determined to try to do better.   For a while he made an effort, but one early morning after having been torn from his blissful dreams by force, it all became too much and he swore at his awakening party. Incensed, one of them complained to the Principal about the disgraceful language of one who purported to be a Christian. He felt that the grievous offence should not go unpunished.

The Principal took a dim view of such bad behaviour and, wishing to nip it in the bud, he summoned the recalcitrant young man.

"Why are you behaving like this in the morning - to the point of swearing?" he remonstrated. "- And you a committed Christian. This is not a good example to your fellow students, is it?"

The young man was penitent. "I'm very sorry, sir," he said. "It's the 'old man'."

The puzzled Principal frowned. "The 'old man'?" he said, "what do you mean, - the 'old man'?"

"Well, sir," explained the student. "Jesus said that when we accept Him as our Saviour, He will create a new nature within us - a 'new man' ; but until we get to Glory, the 'old man' and the 'new man' exist together. You see, sir, my trouble is that the 'old man' wakes up first!"

These days at the start of the nineteen fifties were exciting for the Christian world. With the end of the Second World War, people began to recover with optimism for the future. During the war, the churches filled with desperate people praying for deliverance, and now a grateful momentum continued. A wave of fervour swept across the country from America, and young people everywhere - growing up in a broadly Christian society - joined in. It was a time of vibrant Youth Fellowships, crowded 'Youth For Christ' meetings and extensive evangelism. Billy Graham began his world-wide crusades and people responded in droves. Nowadays, our young people are growing up in a pagan society which scorns Christianity. The result is a crime-ridden environment in which our children have no moral example to follow and no hope for the future. Although the Christians at my college were the minority, we did not have to fight against a tide of ridicule and opposition as a Christian child in school or college would struggle with today. Many may not have wanted to take part, but they respected our beliefs. This became evident in the freedom to meet together we enjoyed at college.

In those days, the official line meant the separation of the sexes, and therefore most schools admitted only one sex. But in rare 'co-educational' cases with boys and girls admitted together, they were expected to behave decorously at all times. To ensure this at our college, free time activities could only be undertaken separately. Boys' groups and girls' groups existed for nearly everything, with girl-boy relationships under especial control.

It had to be admitted that if boys and girls were educated together than they would inevitably become romantically involved, so in order to avoid excesses, firm rules resulted. To this end, therefore, if you were 'going out' with a girl, you could either sit in the hall at a table and talk, or you could take advantage of one hour at dinner time when you could walk down the drive together. At all time overt physical contact was frowned upon. Young people nowadays would find the picture very funny indeed - to see prim and proper couples sitting at tables gazing into each other's eyes and conversing formally, or the pairs wandering up and down the drive for the length of the one 'meeting' hour!

Our Christian Fellowship held a mid-week evening prayer meeting in addition to the morning ones. The only place available for us to meet was in the typing building when all the typewriters had fallen silent. Against all expectations we got permission to meet there and pray. We felt this to be a triumph for Christianity because the authorities were trusting the boys and girls to meet together without supervision and to behave properly.

The meeting grew to such a degree that by the end of my college time we actually held it in the Assembly Hall! And it was a prayer meeting - not just an excuse for boys and girls to get together! The proof showed in the answered prayers - young people coming to know the Lord so that their lives were changed.

The continued enthusiasm led us to invite the folk from the Shrewsbury Christian Fellowship to join us for a 'Celebration'. Young people from all the various churches around the area made up the Fellowship, and they welcomed the chance to praise God together.

On the night, they poured into our college in droves - some cycled, a few crowded into 'old bangers', many walked, but one group acquired a farm tractor and collected people all along the way! By the time it reached us, folk hung all over it! It was a wonderful evening which would not have been heard of a few years before. How sad it is that young people nowadays have little else to do but watch violent videos or get into mischief.

I must have stood out as particularly keen amongst all the other students because the Principal chose me to attend two Student Christian Movement Schools' Conferences. Perhaps he hoped I would learn a little more restraint, and although I was flattered to be chosen, I did feel a little apprehensive of the venture. They were both held in school buildings during the holidays, and I knew that before I could function independently, I would each time have to get to know the layout of the buildings.

The students at the conferences were gleaned mainly from the Higher Education end of the spectrum - which accounted for the inclusion of our college. I found myself, therefore , the only blind person attending.

This meant that I would be dependent upon the others - strangers at that - to help me familiarise with the buildings. This was all very well, but sighted people tend to try to 'make allowances' for the blind, and I did not want that. There are a variety of facts I need to know when I visit a building new to me. Mainly, I need to find out where all the obstacles are situated - fire extinguishers, tables, chairs, surplus wardrobes or similar furniture often stored on landings. Then I would need to know where the bathrooms and toilets were situated in relation to my dormitory, and where the dining room and any other necessary rooms could be located.

People are very kind. They want to help, and experience told me that when sighted people show you around a house, not many will show you what comes in between a bedroom and a bathroom. They will take you down the centre of the landing so as to avoid the obstacles, or they will tend to remove things if you go a bit too close to them - "Oh, let me take that out of your way," they will say. This is not what I want. I would rather nothing should be altered, but that they would give me a moment or two to take account of the setting, then after that I will be able to get around perfectly well.

When I arrived at the school near Matlock where the conference was being held, I found out first about the agenda for the day. I noted that there would be a free afternoon and that most people would opt to go out for a walk. My new acquaintances cordially invited me to go along, but I refused politely. This would be my reconnoitring time. While they were all out, I took myself around the whole building and quietly noted everything. By the time they came back I was satisfied. I could be self-sufficient and for the rest of the conference I could concentrate on more important things.

If I have time to familiarise with my surroundings, I find I can avoid most accidents. I could not arrange things so conveniently when I once visited an old people's complex. I arrived by taxi, having been told that some kind of cord hung on the wall in the entrance hall, and when pulled, it would summon the warden. I searched for it everywhere but couldn't find it at all. As I concentrated on running my hands over the walls, I came up against a small table covered with a cloth. Somehow I caught the cloth and the whole thing went over.

To my horror I realised that a vase of flowers had been standing on it, but that now the flowers were strewn all over the floor! As I tried to retrieve them, I was relieved to discover that the vase still remained in one piece, and that the flowers were imitation ones, so they had not been in water! I quickly replaced the table and picked up the flowers, trying to be sure that I didn't miss any. I eventually located the bell-cord, and no-one seemed to be any the wiser about my accident.

The greatest surprise to me at the conference occurred in finding that I felt like a 'fish out of water' - not because of my blindness, but because I was an evangelical Christian. When I came to understand Jesus as my Saviour and Lord, it became natural to me that others should want to learn about Him as I had - in fact, I thought everyone would jump at the chance to discover Jesus - once they had been told. This made me 'evangelical'. The revelation that others were not as enthusiastic as I came as quite a shock, and it made me very sad that people sometimes found my enthusiasm irritating.

But when I met up with the other Christians at the conference, I learned that a very different side to Christianity existed. A sober, quiet, more academic side. This was all right in its way, but it disappointed me that there appeared to be no desire to tell the good news to others, and no obvious love for the Lord which would result in changed lives. It seemed to me that they were missing the point. Jesus died for everyone, and that since the Bible says 'Believe on the Lord Jesus Christ and you will be saved'[1] then it is very important to tell others what they are missing - otherwise they will be lost.

I just couldn't understand - and still can't - why people who know this vital fact which is emphasised all through the Bible, don't go straight out and tell as many people about it as possible.

During discussion groups I found myself speaking up when everyone else seemed dumb.

"Why did Jesus rise again?" prompted the young lady leader. "What was the point of the resurrection?"

After a moment's silence, I had to say something.

"Well, the point is that everything hangs on that," I offered, mystified at such a silly question. "Without it Calvary wouldn't be valid." It all seemed perfectly obvious to me, but the leader was quite excited.

"Oh, good! Good!" she exclaimed. "We'll put that.," she grabbed a pencil and scribbled enthusiastically: "'The cross made valid'". Then looking hopefully at me again she asked, "What else would you say?"

Since she asked, I told her. "It vindicated not only the life and death of Jesus Christ........."

"Oh, hang on! Hang on!" she said, and wrote, 'It vindi-cated.............'

"But," I said, after a pause so that she could quote me precisely, "It also vindicated the sure prophecy that He would be coming back to earth."

"Pardon?" she said, looking up with a puzzled expression.

I repeated what I had said, and she wrote it down quietly. Afterwards she met me privately.

"I'm very interested in what you said. Do you think Jesus is really coming back?"

"Let me show you," I offered, and I quoted chapter and verse of the New Testament verses I learned when a child attending Sunday School. I didn't know them all, but I knew enough, and she seemed quite bowled over by the revelation. She had no idea at all that Jesus would return one day.

It all served to teach me that Christians came in more than one type. When I discovered Jesus Christ, I assumed that everyone else who knew him would have learned the same things as I and be equally keen and 'evangelistic'. I found it distressing that there were some who knew about Jesus, but had done absolutely nothing about that knowledge. I couldn't believe that they could be satisfied to miss anything so important. By the end of my time in college, I learned more than how to tune a piano!

The final tuning test at the end of the course took place in London. We all felt it to be an auspicious occasion which would make or break our futures, and we discussed it avidly, trying to predict and prepare for what we would be asked to do.

"They are bound to give us a piano which is flat," one of my friends mused anxiously.

"Of course," said another, "but how flat? I bet it'll be miles down and it'll be the dickens of a job to get it up to pitch."

We all mumbled agreement, dreading the task ahead.

A complete surprise awaited me when the day finally came. Instead of the anticipated very flat piano, I had to tune one which was sharp! It would have to be taken down to pitch! It stopped me in my tracks for a moment, but I soon collected myself and got on with the job. It held no real fears for me - I knew I could do it easily, and I loved every minute I spent with pianos, whether sharp or flat!

I passed the test with honours and eventually received my diploma in a presentation from the great conductor Sir Adrian Boult, at the college's annual Speech Day some time later.

I was now fitted to go out into the world and earn my own living.

CHAPTER TWO
TUNING IN

WHEN I FIRST LEFT college, I was confident that I would find work. To begin with, I knew myself to be a 'natural' tuner, and I had passed my exams with honours. The Birmingham Workshops would very likely be willing to start me off. The Workshops existed to give 'sheltered' work to the blind, and they were, indeed, willing to take me on. I started soon after my twenty-first birthday.

Although rather low pay, it did constitute a regular income at a time when tuners began to experience a hard time with television becoming popular, and a good company of characters were content to spend the whole of their working lives with the Workshops. I knew it would not suit me for long, however - I wanted to be independent, but I was very grateful for the help and caring attitude I received from my employers at the start of my career.

All the tuners were musicians, and most looked on life with a sort of 'tongue in cheek' humour. We would turn up every morning to hand over the takings from the day before, and to pick up our calls for the new day. As a 'new boy', my first problem concerned getting to know my way around. I had no wish to waste precious earning time wandering about the streets looking for the places where I was supposed to go.

My colleagues used to help me out in this respect. Most of them were 'old stagers' who knew the geography of Birmingham inside out, and they taught me everything. They would say 'you go this way, then that way......' but they used to include the sort of detail that a sighted person wouldn't think of.

"When you turn right, you must be careful because there's a double curb there - you go down one step, and then another."

"...You'll pass three dips in the road - they're not roads with curbs, but entrances. At the fourth entrance, you'll be there."

There is a saying that if a blind person gives you directions, you'll never go wrong.

There have been times since then when I have been sitting on a bus, and someone has said, "Excuse me, sir, will you tell me when we get to the valley.........?" and I have said, "Okay, I'll let you know." I can usually tell where I am at any one point. A blind person is very aware of left and right turns, roundabouts and traffic islands, hills and bridges. Then the wheel sounds change with the kind of road surface, or as the buildings differ on either side, the sounds bounce off the different surfaces and it is easy to tell where you are if you know the area.

I heard a story about a lady who took a journey on a bus, but the route the bus travelled was one of the longest in the city. It went all the way from Handsworth Wood in the north of the city to South Yardley in the south. It meant crossing the entire city and naturally took a long time.

The lady got on at Handsworth Wood, and as this was in the days when the buses had a crew of two, she asked the conductor if the bus went to Small Heath. A huge, jovial black man, the conductor had a keen sense of humour.

"Cer-tan-lee, ma'am," he said cheerfully. "I will sure-lee tell you when we get there."

They set off, but she was anxious, and after what seemed to her to be a long time, she asked again, "Er, excuse me, this bus does go to Small Heath, doesn't it?"

"Don' you worry, ma'am," the conductor assured her, "I won't forget to let you know when you am there."

They went on a bit further, but she couldn't believe it could take so long to get to her destination, so in desperation she asked again. "We haven't passed Small Heath, have we?   This bus is really going there, isn't it?"

Now the conductor had had enough. He said, "You jus' come with me, ma'am," and taking her by the arm, he led her to the front of the bus where the driver, who was an Irishman, sat in a cab on his own, separated from the passengers by a window. The large black man knocked on the window.

"Ben," he asked the driver, patiently, "would you tell this lady here that this bus is definite-lee going to Small Heath?"

"Sure it is," confirmed the driver. "We'll be there is about fifteen minutes, sure we will."

The conductor turned to the woman, and in a strained voice said, "There you are, ma'am. Are you satisfied? Now you has it in black and white!"

It's a pity that buses don't still have the two-man crews. They used to be very helpful to blind people - particularly when you wanted to know where you were going. Nowadays with the driver usually cut off from the passengers, and with the rule that they should not be disturbed by being spoken to, it's much more difficult for us.

Some of the conductors were personalities in themselves. I remember one on a route I took regularly who would rhyme his words as he called out each stop.

"Brook Lane - Here again!" he would sing out happily. Or "School Road - Well I'll be blowed!" But as we passed the bus depot, his call would be "Bus Depot - Sons of Rest!" He was a real character and brightened our day as we waited to see what he would say next. Travelling by bus is not half so interesting nowadays.

Another story used to be told about one of the lads who waited some time at the stop for a bus. As it was rush hour, when the bus arrived not a spare seat remained. Usually the conductors would try to get one or two more squeezed in, but on this particular morning the Asian conductor knew that an Inspector hovered around to check up on him. So he could do no more than let people off. The crowd waiting at the stop surged forward, but the conductor was adamant.

"I'm sorry," he shouted, "I cannot take anymore. I am ram-jam full!"

So our man waiting called out to him, "I don't care what your name is, I want to get on your bus!"

One of the characters at the Birmingham Workshops was Tommy. A 'Brummy' born and bred, he had a very thick accent;

smoked like a chimney and told very tall stories. One morning he came in with the money from the previous day's tuning in an envelope and gave it to the foreman who counted it out, but discovered that it was not complete.

"Tommy," he said, puzzled, "you're two pounds short."

"Oh, yeah," began Tommy confidently, "I'm very sorry about that, but y'see, I 'ad this money in me pocket with me 'andherchief, an' when I sneezed I pulled me 'anky out so quick that some of the money fell out an' went down a drain....."

There was no way the foreman could prove otherwise, but we all knew that it was more likely Tommy had popped in the pub for a quick one on his way home!

Another time Tommy did not turn up on time for work in the morning. The foreman asked us if we knew what had happened to him, but we didn't, and it was only when we were all ready to go off that Tommy came hurrying in.

"Where have you been?" asked the irritated foreman. "Why are you so late?"

"Well, now," Tommy began with a hint of anguish in his voice, "you're not goin' to believe this, but there I was waitin' for this bus, and when it came, d'you know what?" We all muttered 'no' as we waited for the inevitable punch line.

"Well, the blinkin' wheel stopped right on me foot - on me shoe! I couldn't move! They said, 'come on Tommy, the bus is waitin', but I told 'em "I can't get on this bus until you move it off me foot!"

The frustrated foreman waved him off without a word. It was no use arguing with him when he came up with stories as original as that!

When we all got together sometimes, the stories got even more outrageous. A typical one which looked like being passed into folklore came from the time when there were horses and carts in the streets. Apparently a policeman had come across a dead horse in Conybere Street, Balsall Heath. Since there were no pocket radios in those days, he needed to go to the nearest police telephone and ring the station.

"Sarge," he said, "there's a horse here in the street that's died in the shafts."

"Where are you?" inquired the sergeant.

"Conybere Street," replied the policeman.

"Okay, just make your report out as usual."

"Right-O, Sarge," said the copper, and rang off.

Three quarters of an hour later he rang again. He said, "Sarge, you know that horse that died in the shafts?"

"Yes," replied the sergeant, "what about it?"

"Well, we managed to move it round to New Street."

"What for?" asked the puzzled sergeant.

"'Cos I can spell that!" explained the policeman.

The characters at the Birmingham Workshops had all been tuning for years when I arrived as a twenty-one year old.

I soon found out that I had to earn not only my money, but also my reputation as a tuner. People tended to feel that an experienced man could be trusted, whereas a younger man would not have gained sufficient experience to be any good.

One of the first customers I went to from the Workshops was a very fine violinist who knew a great deal about music. When I arrived his wife gave me a message from him. "I hope you won't mind," she began rather tentatively, "but my husband has asked if you would please use his tuning fork to tune the piano."

"Certainly," I replied, thinking that mine would be perfectly adequate for the job. However, when she passed it to me, I realised it to be an 'A' fork. Although exactly the same pitch as my 'C' fork, it was simply tuned to 'A' instead of 'C'.

"He would like the piano tuned to A440," added the wife, and I knew then that this customer knew exactly what he was talking about. As the leader of the Orchestra Da Camera, a well-known Midland orchestra - he would naturally use an 'A' for tuning. It would actually have made no difference to the tuning for me to use either of the tuning forks, but I complied with the request.

Just before I had finished, my musician customer came home. "I hope you got my message," he asked anxiously. "Yes, I did," I replied, "and I found it very interesting."

"Oh, why was that?" he asked, surprised.

"Well, we use a 'C' fork usually, as you know, but I found it a whole new experience to begin the scale from a different perspective."

When I had finished, he ran his hands over the keys. "Wonderful!" he said, enthusiastically. "You've done a very good job here. I hope you'll come again."

I did, but not only that - when I left the firm to launch out on my own, he insisted on remaining with me to the embarrassment my employers and myself at the Workshops.

I found the same 'A' fork preference when I tuned for the BBC and the Midland Light Orchestra. As the members of the orchestra came in for rehearsal, they would see my 'A' tuning fork on the piano and say, "Oh, you use an 'A' fork, do you? That's good - it's the same as ours."

Somehow it satisfied them to know that I tuned from 'A' although I knew it would make no difference at all. In the end I used to alternate - 'C' one time, 'A' the next. It gave me variety, but I smugly noticed that they were always pleased with my tuning, no matter which fork I had used!

At the other end of the scale - if you'll pardon the pun - are the customers who haven't a clue! On my first visit to another lady, she was quite puzzled.

"We don't know what's the matter," she moaned, "My daughter has a clarinet, and her friend who can also play wants to help her, but the clarinet won't go with the piano at all."

I had only to sound one note to discover that the piano was about a semi-tone flat. No wonder it didn't fit! It must have sounded excruciating!

"The reason is because your piano is at a different pitch from the clarinet," I explained patiently.

"Oh," she said, sadly, "is the clarinet wrong then?"

"Why do you say that?" I pressed.

"Because your firm has been tuning this piano for some years, so it can't be wrong, can it?"

Knowing absolutely nothing about music, she assumed that different instruments necessarily played at different pitches, and that there was no hope for her daughter and friend to be able to play together.

I knew, however, that it simply meant that the tuner had not bothered to get the piano up to standard pitch. He just took the easy way out and tuned it from where he had left it. It involved me in something of a diplomatic exercise. I could not criticise the other tuners. "Well, look," I said, thinking fast. "I think it's just that this piano has been at this particular pitch for so long, they thought they ought not to disturb it, but if you want the piano at clarinet pitch, I can do it for you."

This was another customer who came with me when I left the Workshops, although I would never have tried to take them deliberately.

Of course, there are many people who have no idea about pitch, and most of the time it would make no difference to them if their pianos were not tuned to standard pitch - so long as they did not sound discordant. But that is not good enough for me, and as I go around, I like to try to educate my customers.

I went to tune the piano of a minister, once, and when I tried it, I said, "Do you know your piano is telling lies?"

"What do you mean?" he asked, intrigued.

"Well, what's that note?" I said, as I played one.

"It's 'C'," he said.

"Yes, it is indeed the note 'C'," I agreed, but added, "only it's sounding 'B'. Therefore your piano is telling fibs!"

As the minister took that in, I went on. "Now, we can't have moral declension in a clergyman's house, can we? I shall have to raise it a complete semi-tone, and that will put it right!"

It is probably a minor matter, (sorry - there's another pun!) but I think there is a morality about piano tuning. If note 'C' is being played when it's actually sounding something else, then it's my job to bring a piano to the pitch in which it was made to be played. If it is flat or sharp, then it's there by default and I don't feel I can leave it like that.

While I'm talking about morals, I have noticed that the whole climate in people's homes has changed in recent years. When I first started tuning, we never ever thought that there could be problems with our being in strange houses. We were welcomed in, and got on with the job we had come to do.

Now it's different. I can pin down the shift in attitudes where they concerned me, to about ten years ago when I rang up to advise a customer about a tuning. It was a policeman's house, and he answered the phone. I suggested a date for the tuning, but he said it would not be convenient.

"You won't be able to come then, because my wife and I are both at work, and my daughter will be at home on her own."

Innocently I said, "Well, that's all right, then, isn't it?"

"No, it isn't," he replied quickly, "my daughter will not let anyone in whom she doesn't know."

I experienced my first pang of embarrassment in this respect at that moment, and I have been wary ever since. The same thing happened again some time later, and on that occasion I mentioned that my wife would be with me, but the customer still did not accept.

But it works the other way round too. Left alone with a determined woman, it would be my word against hers if any misconduct was alleged - and it would be more likely that her word would be believed. The whole moral climate has changed.

I always regard it a privilege to go into people's homes - to be trusted to do as I like with people's precious pianos - it is a wonderful privilege that I would never abuse. Now, however, one has to be so careful.

I went to tune a piano in Leicester some time ago, having been told, "There won't be anyone available to let you in until four o'clock when our daughter gets home from school."

I arrived just after four and the girl answered the door, so I went in. I got settled and started tuning. Then there was another knock on the door and a boy came in. The young girl did not bother to introduce me, but I sensed that he was not a relation.

"If you want me, I'm upstairs," she called, and off they went together. I knew that her mother would not be home until six, and so I found myself in the house with the two young people upstairs together. I felt very uncomfortable and not a little vulnerable. If the girl came to any harm, it might be my word against hers as to the fact that I was not the only male in the house at the time.

Even recently, I went to tune the piano of an elderly lady. As the lady let me in, I closed the door behind me. She then reached over and turned the key in the lock! "You never know who's coming in nowadays," she said, but I was amazed. 'This is real trust,' I thought to myself. 'She's locked me in with her!'

I like it when people trust me, but the whole world seems to run on mistrust now.

I worry because grown ups are teaching children to mistrust everything and everyone. It is quite understandable, but it will have awful effects as they grow up. They will mistrust and be mistrusted in return. I dread to think what they will lead to in later life. Margaret and I were looking for an address a short time ago, and we asked some children if they knew where was such and such a church. "We're not supposed to speak to you, but it's round to the left........" How sad that the world should come to such a state.

Of course, there have always been stories about the visit of the piano tuner/window cleaner or suchlike.........

A woman called the doctor because she had a boil in a very difficult place, but discovered that since the doctor was on holiday, a locum would attend her. At the appropriate time, a knock came on the door and she went to answer it.

"Come in," she said to the man on the step, "I'll be with you in a minute."

Moments later she returned in a state of undress, ready for the doctor.

"No, madam, please!" protested her visitor. "I have only come to tune the piano!"

CHAPTER THREE

IN TUNE WITH
THE CUSTOMERS

I BEGAN TO LEARN how much the customers are dependent upon the integrity of their piano tuner from my very first job. It was in girls' school in Birmingham and I had to tune all the pianos around the building, but after I finished, the Head teacher still wanted me to see one more.

"Would you mind looking at the piano we have in the staff room?" she asked. "You don't need to tune it, but I would be grateful if you would value it for me."

At the first touch I could tell that it was no good at all, but to make sure I took the front off and removed the action so that I could look it over completely. It was total rubbish and needed to be scrapped! But as I investigated the works, I came across eleven pence worth of coins that had been dropped inside at some time.

When I returned to the Head teacher, she asked hopefully, "How much do you think it's worth, then?"

Putting the coins in her hand, I told her my honest opinion. "It's worth minus eleven pence!" I said, and left her to dispose of the piano and the coins!

As tuners we often came up against some horrendous pianos! Their owners seemed to expect that with a tug on a string here, or a tweak there, we could change it from a beast to a beauty! Sometimes we could, but more often the task would be impossible, and not a little dangerous........

During my first days in the Birmingham Workshops, an old wooden framed piano was brought in of the kind made in the eighteenth or nineteenth centuries.

We learned that only in later years were pianos built with iron frames - the frames being the part onto which the strings are stretched.   Before this, most pianos had frames made of wood. Today's iron frames give the strings much greater stability. Wooden framed pianos, however, still retain a residue of moisture and are therefore more susceptible to temperature and humidity.

The old piano brought into the workshop was one like this, and would need a major overhaul. It had stood for a long time in a living room where, during the winter, a fire always burned in the grate. Even at night the fire had been stacked up with coal so that it burned gently until morning, so the piano had never been subjected to cold at all. It stood comfortably against the wall, nicely cushioned from any changes of climate.

Our workroom was not so thoughtfully kept at an even temperature. Sometimes it would drop a full twenty degrees or more at night, and when we came in in the morning, the cold pinched our fingers as we tried to start our work. Into this desperate change in atmosphere, the piano was brought one evening, so that it would be ready for us to begin work on it the next day.

When we came in to the workshop in the morning, the foreman could not believe his eyes! Where the old piano had stood, lay a mangled pile of wood and strings! The strings must have contracted in the cold, and the vulnerable wooden frame gave way under the pressure, pulling the piano completely apart! The noise when it happened must have been incredible, and if we had been in the room at the time, it would have been very dangerous. One string breaking can cause a nasty lash injury, but for all of them to go at once, could have been horrific!

I was therefore cautious one day when I went to tune a very old piano in Market Harborough.

Uncharacteristically, I left Andy, my guide dog to settle down on the lawn in the garden on a lovely sunny day, while I went in to the front room to deal with the piano. Usually Andy would lie at my feet, but for some reason , he remained outside. I gave the piano an initial inspection. It was not a good prospect.

"Were you expecting this piano brought up to standard pitch?" I asked the owner guardedly. He replied that correct pitch was necessary, because as a musician, he needed to play it with other instrumentalists.

"I don't think I can do it," I told him. "It might crack under the pressure."

"Well," said my customer, "it really is no good to me unless it is brought up to concert pitch. Can you try it?"

"Well I could........" I said, "but it would be make or break - literally. If it holds, then it will be very good. But if it doesn't, then the piano will be completely wrecked."

The man considered the implications for a moment, then made his decision.

"Right," he said. "Do it. Make or break. I'll take the risk."

I set to work very carefully. I had no wish to be sliced by a breaking string.

All went well for a while, and I hoped it might be successful. Then suddenly the front of the piano heaved forwards. It 'exploded' like a rifle shot and the back lifted upwards and hit the wall. I put out my hands to protect myself as I felt half the piano lurch towards me, expecting to be injured by flaying strings and darting wooden shards. It was quite terrifying. I could feel the whole piano opening up - the frame twisting grotesquely with the pressure of the taut strings. When it stopped, I sat for a second or two breathing a sigh of relief and collecting myself. I, at least, remained in one piece. I was also relieved that Andy had not been in the room. He would have been very frightened, and maybe even injured.

My customer rushed in when he heard the explosion. Perhaps he felt relieved to discover me still alive after thinking the worst, but his reaction to the pile of debris that had once been his piano was very restrained. He had been warned of the possible outcome, so not much could be said. All that could be done now would be to dispose of the rubbish and think towards a new piano!

I thought I had no illusions as to the condition of some of the pianos that I would be asked to tune. I saw plenty of disastrous ones during my three years' training at college and therefore assumed that all piano tuners would have the same enthusiastic attitude to tuning as my own.

I certainly had no illusions about the owners of the pianos that I would tune. I accepted that there would be much ignorance and that people would rely on me completely to do a good job. I knew that by and large, most people could not tell whether their piano had been tuned well or not. Only in the most extreme cases would an owner notice the difference, or perhaps if he or she happened to be a good musician. If, however, the piano were tuned regularly, then on the whole untrained ears would not notice much change. But I never ceased to be shocked when I discovered the condition in which some tuners left their pianos.

I visited one lady for the first time, and tried out the keys to see what condition the piano was in. I noticed immediately that the octaves at the top end of the keyboard were much flatter than the rest, and mentioned it to the lady.

"Oh, yes," she said. "That was because the last tuner left it to go and get his bus!" I could hardly believe what I heard!

Another customer did not allow herself to be so deceived. When she called me in to help, she explained why she wanted to change tuners. As a cello teacher used to tuning the strings of her cello, she was quite knowledgeable and certainly knew something about how long a piano with its numerous strings should take to tune. She was therefore surprised when her previous piano tuner told her he had finished the job in about twenty minutes.

"Have you done it then?" she asked, puzzled.

"Oh, yes," he replied, putting on his coat. "It's all finished."

The lady tested some notes. "But the scale is not tempered properly," she protested. "Listen to that fifth - it's wobbling about like anything." The tuner had not bargained on an expert. He decided to tell the truth.

"Well, I'm playing at a gig tonight. I just haven't time to do any more"

It was the last time he tuned her piano, and soon after, I got the job. I learned a good deal about people and their pianos from one of the tutors at college - a Mr. Whitton who had also previously been a teacher at my school. We always knew when he arrived in the building because he smoked a lot and the smell of his cigarettes permeated the whole place!

Mr. Whitton was quite a character and would regale us with stories about his piano tuning days. He would tell us that we did not just tune pianos, but customers - we had to keep them 'tuned in'. He gave us essentially practical advice.

"You will be offered tea or coffee," he told us. "Always opt for tea." We all understood and noted the advice, because coffee in those days was a luxury item and very expensive. It would be more diplomatic to take the tea.

"Always say what you mean," he continued, and elaborated. "If you need the toilet, say so." Puzzled, we waited for his explanation of this obvious fact. It came in the recounting of a story. "I knew one young man," he said, lighting up another cigarette, "who was strangely embarrassed about specifying that he needed to go to the toilet. He simply asked if he could 'wash his hands'.

"Of course," said the accommodating customer, and disappeared for a moment only to return with a bowl of water, some soap and a towel!"

It was Mr. Whitton who pointed out some of the ignorance we would come up against in our customers.

He told us that once he worked on a particularly out of tune piano. It was so bad that it needed extensive work and he spent a long time on it. When he left it at last, he felt quite satisfied that it was as good as he could make it.

A day or two later he received a letter from the customer. 'Thank you for tuning my piano,' it said, 'but would you please come and put the 'bells' back in?' The twangy, out of tune notes had sounded like cracked bells to her and she thought something was now missing!

Mr. Whitton told us of another man who thought he knew about tuning and could therefore save himself the expense of bringing in a tuner to fix a broken string on his piano. He looked at the inside of the piano and found out how the strings were fixed so decided that he could see to the job himself. He removed the string from the piano, and went off to his local music shop. After showing the broken string and asking for a replacement, he added knowledgeably, "Would you please tune it for me, then I'll put it on the piano myself."!

Tuning pianos is, of course, a very technical art that takes several years of intensive training to complete successfully. However, I too, have known people who have bought themselves a tuning lever and then launched themselves on their defenceless pianos, thinking that all they had to do was to tighten or loosen the strings to achieve a reasonable tune and so save themselves expense. I suppose tightening and loosening strings is what happens basically, but there is a very great deal more to it than that.

To begin with, the student has to be trained to listen to the infinitesimal changes of pitch that will mean the difference between harmony and discord. A tuning fork will help to set the pitch, and each student comes to regard this two-pronged 'fork' as vital equipment for the job. When tapped - usually on the body to avoid possible damage to the fork and to avoid unnecessary vibrations - the tuning fork will vibrate at an exact frequency and so sound a perfect note. The average person will not notice any difference between various tuning-fork performances, but with training and a good ear, the student can recognise variations.

It might be possible to tune a piano without using a tuning-fork, but if the piano is to be kept in peak condition, then the tuning-fork will act as a kind of 'stethoscope' with which the tuner will be able to discover precisely how the piano has fared since his last visit - whether it has gone sharp or flat. Then he can act accordingly, and tune the piano as near perfectly as he can manage.

One day I went to a house to tune a piano for the first time, and used my tuning fork which told me that the piano was a complete semi-tone flat.

"Ah," I said to the lady, "I'll have to raise it."

She looked alarmed. "Oh, dear," she said, "my husband doesn't get in 'til six - you won't be able to lift it all on your own." 'Raising' in her mind meant something totally different!

Sometimes when I go to tune a piano I find that I have a lot more work to do than just tuning the strings. When this happens, my schedule is thrown into disarray. One unexpected delay however that set me back several hours, was not so much the result of a faulty piano, but a faulty customer!

I had been asked to tune the piano of an elderly lady, whom I had known for some years. I didn't see her very often, but when I happened to be ministering in her area, I would usually tune her piano because she found difficulty in finding a local tuner.

The lady with whom I was staying very kindly took me to the elderly lady's home and arranged to collect me at lunchtime, and so I began the work. There was much to do as I had to remove the action - that is, the frame with all the moving parts such as the hammers and dampers, etc. I carefully placed the action frame on the floor beside me.

Some time later, when I was approaching the end of the job, the elderly lady came back in the room to bring me a cup of coffee.

But the action frame barred her way, and instead of going round it, she simply walked all over it - hammers, dampers, tapes, springs and all! Several of the parts were quite ruined and it took me several more hours and a missed lunch to get them all repaired!

At college the more experienced students were very hard on the new boys. We would hear someone in a practice room trying to get a piano right, and with a tuning fork of a slightly different pitch we would very gently put our fork on the door so that it would hum away.......... The poor student wouldn't understand why he couldn't get it right! He would be thrown completely!

Each note of a piano is made by a hammer hitting not one, but three strings, and these three strings have to be tuned to sound in complete unison - without any distortion at all. It occurred to me that this fact is really quite a good analogy of the Godhead - Father, Son and Holy Spirit, three in One working together with no distortion.

The next important step in the tuning is to do the foundation - or scale - using the middle twelve semi-tones - the twelve notes closest together in the middle of the keyboard. These have to be tuned in ratio with one another and is called 'Tempering the Scale' As I learned about this I immediately thought about the city with twelve foundations which I read about in the book of Revelation at the end of the Bible.[2] God built His Holy City on firm foundations, and when I tune a piano, I build my tuning on the firm foundation of a twelve note 'tempered scale'. If this is not done properly, then there can be no harmony.

In the nineteen fifties and sixties we did not have the modern translations of the Bible, and I had read in my Authorised Version in 1 Corinthians, chapter 12, where St. Paul explains that as Christians with varied gifts we should all work together for the good of all.

God hath tempered the body together......[3] it said. We are told that we have to 'temper' our differences so that we can work together in harmony.

I was struck by these analogies and stored them in my mind for future use if I needed to help someone to a better understanding of the work of God.

The well-tempered piano will bring harmony - its called 'equal temperament' - and that is just the way a good church works. We are all different, but we have to be 'tempered' to bring harmony. J.S.

Bach demonstrated the effect when he wrote his 48 preludes and fugues for the well-tempered Klavier (or keyboard) set in each of all the major and minor keys possible.

Pitch is a profoundly interesting subject, and one that has fascinated me since my early days. It always amazes me how the pitch of a piece of music can affect the way it is sung.

I remember a man with a tenor voice similar to that of Harry Secombe, who rang me one day to arrange a time for me to tune his piano. When I got there, I tested middle 'C' with a tuning fork and found it to be a semi-tone lower than it should have been. "Oh, dear," I said, "that doesn't sound too good."

"What's the matter, Bach?" he said in a rich Welsh accent.

"Your piano's at the wrong pitch," I explained.

The man paused, puzzled. "I'm a tenor, you know," he said, as though that would account for the discrepancy.

"Yes," I said, "but put it this way: If I raise your piano to the correct pitch, you would be only half the tenor you thought you were this morning - only a fiver!"

During my years as an evangelist and accompanist, I have often been struck by the way in which the congregation's mood can vary even from verse to verse in the singing of a hymn. They might be sad or negative, tired or depressed, and if I simply modulate to a higher key, it can make all the difference to the singing - and even the understanding of what they are singing. The pitch of the hymn can alter the whole mood. It is also a strange fact that it is harder to sing higher in the mornings, so whenever I am playing for congregational singing, I always pitch the songs a semi-tone lower before lunch!

For me, playing a piano has always been a deeply spiritual experience. From my earliest days it has been something that touches me in my innermost being and reaches deep into my soul. For this reason I have always found it difficult to play as part of a worship group to lead congregational singing.

Playing with a group means responding one to another and not to one's own instinct. It is very difficult to define, but I have to be free to respond to the congregation's mood, and I feel I have let them down if I cannot respond to their needs. I find the whole area of pitch and spirituality very interesting indeed.

It was all impressed on me very simply but firmly, when I listened in the mid-fifties to one of the first Billy Graham relays in

Birmingham. Ted Smith, the pianist, started the final hymn Just as I Am in a particular key. The moment was very emotional as hundreds of people all over the country began to leave their seats and walk down to the front of the various halls where they were listening in response to the call to follow Jesus Christ. Ted played sensitively and beautifully, ensuring that nothing would detract from the important moment of decision for so many people. The idea was that gradually the relay would fade and the local organist in our hall would take over while the people were coming forward.

Unfortunately, our organist could only play from music, and Ted Smith had played 'Just as I Am' in a different key to the one printed in the church music copy. The resulting sudden jarring as one key changed drastically and discordantly to another, shattered the atmosphere completely. This constituted my first real lesson in the association of the spiritual with the practical where music is concerned.

●●●

I seem to be asked quite frequently if I can tune dreadful, worn out pianos, but rather less frequently, I see beautiful instruments that have not been tuned or looked after properly. Whenever I see one of these neglected beauties, I am compelled to try to do something about it.

I came across one such magnificent specimen when I visited a piano showroom in Cardiff with a friend. Here was a Feurich - a superb piano made in Western Germany - with a gorgeous tone but somewhat out of tune.

"May I try this piano?" I asked the assistant.

"Certainly," he replied, hopefully. The piano was an expensive one which, I learned later, had been in stock for some time.

As soon as I touched it, I felt sorry for it. With a magnificent tone, it was obviously a beautifully made piano, but just a little out of tune. It really should have been kept in peak condition. Then it would have the ability to enthral. It was such a shame.

"How do you like it?" asked the assistant, not hearing any cries of delight at the magic sounds that he knew the piano could produce.

"It's lovely, but it's out of tune," I ventured, and then added, "If you will permit me to tune it for you tomorrow, I'll sell it for you."

A little taken aback, the assistant surprisingly agreed.

I wondered why they did not have their own tuner. I would have expected a reputable shop to make sure all their stock was kept in good condition. This man did not know me at all, so had no idea what kind of a tuner I would be.

The next day I duly presented myself at the shop, to be greeted with surprise. "Oh, good! You've come to tune it then?" said the assistant I spoke to the day before.

"Yes, I have, and I will do it if you still want me to," I told him.

"Sure, go ahead" he agreed, hoping, I suspect, that I had not forgotten the second part of my offer. When I left later, leaving one of the best pianos to have come my way, I am sure the assistant did not expect to see me again.

As soon as I got home, I telephoned Mr. Williams, one of my customers, whom I knew needed a new piano. I regularly tuned the worn-out wreck which he used for his work as a music teacher.

"I've seen the most gorgeous piano in Cardiff," I enthused. "Why don't you go and have a look at it, and see if you like it?"

"All right," he said, "I have to conduct a choir in Birmingham this weekend, but I'll call into the shop on the way back."

Several days later, I rang to see what he thought about it. His wife answered the phone.

"Yes," Mrs. Williams told me, my husband and I saw the piano on our way to Birmingham. As soon as he sat down to play, I knew he was enchanted with it. All through that weekend he kept saying, 'Oh, what a marvellous piano! I've just got to see it again!'"

"We did go to see it again, and as soon as he sat down to play, he looked at me and sighed. That sigh told me everything! It was a sigh of pure contentment. The Feurich will be delivered to us next week!"

It would be a joy to me too, to look after that lovely instrument.

Incidentally, I recently met Alun, their son, who told me that the day the piano arrived, both he and his father jostled to play it! Alun was supposed to be studying for his A-level examinations, and Mr. Williams kept telling him to go and get on with his studies! "But I want to play the piano, too," protested Alun. They compromised by playing duets far into the night!

Another beautiful piano that I found myself privileged to look after was a Bluthner grand that had belonged to the famous pianist Peter Katin. When he graduated to a Steinway, he sold his Bluthner to a Mr. Maxwell Collins of Northfield, Birmingham. Peter Katin would visit his friend, and give private piano recitals in his large lounge. I would stay on for the recitals, having tuned the Bluthner during the afternoon. I very much enjoyed the close proximity to the eminent pianist which such an evening afforded, although I found myself listening mainly to the tuning, wondering whether it would hold during the fortissimo passages of Brahms, Beethoven or Liszt! Later I was relieved and gratified when Peter Katin complimented me on the excellence of the tuning.

There are two other pianos that stand out in my mind. These were the Bosendorfers used by the BBC in Birmingham. As it happened, the senior school I attended in Carpenter Road, Edgbaston, had a gymnasium which the BBC discovered could double as an excellent studio. They were allowed to take it over now and then to broadcast concerts and other musical events from it, using a small adjacent room as a control room.

As children, we used to have to remain very quiet when the BBC was using the gym, but we were allowed to listen to the concerts on our radios in the dormitories. We found it quite exciting to know that the Midland Light Orchestra together with famous soloists, presenters and musicians were only a little way away, downstairs in our own gym!

When the school's lease on the building eventually ran out, and we were moved to other premises, the BBC took over the whole place and remained there for a number of years while they built and prepared the Pebble Mill studios for radio and television.

It was therefore both exciting and nostalgic for me when, soon after I stepped out on my own as a self-employed tuner, I received a letter from the BBC asking if I would discuss a tuning contract with them.

Margaret and I had not long been married, and I struggled to build up a tuning business. Any contract would be marvellous - let alone one from the BBC! They wanted me to look after their two Bosendorfer concert grands which had been built in 1938, and as this was the nineteen-sixties, they were getting to the end of their lives. They would need sensitive and expert handling.

I felt quite overawed as I walked into the Carpenter Road studios. Not only was I beginning my very first contract - a prestigious one with the BBC - but very strangely, I was returning to the place where I spent a large chunk of my school days.

I knew the building well, and the memories came flooding back as I made my way to the gym - down the corridor, turn right and straight on down to the end. But everything appeared different when I went in. Now the gym was full of complicated equipment. I picked my way carefully through a spaghetti maze of wires and leads attached to microphones, amplifiers and speakers. I went gingerly - I had no wish to bring an expensive microphone crashing to the floor on my first day!

I loved tuning the Bosendorfers and the contract heightened my confidence and helped to establish me as a tuner in my own right, although advertising the fact that one worked for the BBC was not allowed. I also got to know quite a lot of the BBC personnel and personalities in my regular trips to Carpenter Road.

On one occasion I had just finished tuning the pianos ready for the 'Breakfast Special' show to be broadcast on the 'Light Programme' - as the rough equivalent to Radio Two was called in those days. Gilbert conducted the orchestra, and he and the rest of the musicians were just coming in, together with Harold Rich who would play the piano.

"Would you like to stay in to the recording?" Mr. Winter asked me.

"I'd love to," I answered enthusiastically.

"Will your dog be all right?" Mr. Winter questioned, knowing that any undue noise in the studio during recording would cause a great deal of inconvenience.

"She'll be as good as gold, I can promise you that," I assured him, and settled Donna down at my feet with a pat.

All through the recording, Donna never moved, and afterwards Mr. Winter came over to us. "Oh, you are a good dog!" he said, giving Donna an affectionate pat and warm hug. "You're one of the best listeners we've ever had!"

CHAPTER FOUR
SEEING EYES

LOOKING BACK, IT SEEMED to me at first rather strange that nobody working in the Birmingham workshops ever thought of applying for a guide dog. I don't recall anyone ever discussing the possibility with us at school or college, either - which seems amazing under the circumstances. Some of us did carry white canes, but most were too proud to use one - myself included. I suppose the lack of information regarding guide dogs would have been because they were a comparatively new phenomenon in those days, having only been introduced into this country in 1931.

However, several incidents turned my mind to thinking about whether I should consider requesting a dog. Once, when I was walking along Corporation Street in Birmingham, I inadvertently bumped into a newspaper seller. He had apparently been moving about the pavement, trying to persuade people to buy, and I could not anticipate his movements. He turned on me furiously, fists at the ready.

"You wanna make anythin' of it, Mate?" he shouted angrily.

"I'm sorry, I can't see," I said quickly.

"You should carry a white stick, then!" he countered, not in the least mollified by my answer - and although a bit quick tempered, he was right, really.

Lampposts were also something of a hazard. Being comparatively thin, they are easy to hit if your hands are not searching for them - and if you are not feeling ahead with a stick, of course. And I didn't search for them often. I was a very confident walker. I would career about all over the place, making few allowances for the fact that I couldn't see, and I suppose remained fairly trouble free on the whole.

But I had to think a little harder after several falls, the last of which frightened me enough to prompt a reappraisal of my situation. I was making my way down a street when I suddenly fell down an unguarded manhole.

Thankfully I did not fall very far, so I was not badly hurt, but it gave me a bad shock and pulled me up with a start in more ways than one!

Although I perhaps ought to have made something of the fact that the manhole was not adequately protected, my mind, instead, turned towards making sure that such a thing never happened again. A guide dog might be the answer.

There would be no certainty of my being granted a dog. A great many considerations have to be taken into account before trainers will allow any dog to be released into a new owner's home. For a start, there are problems if you are a piano tuner.

A dog functions better in predictable situations. He is not like a human who has an almost unlimited capacity to think out solutions and change his behaviour or actions to suit any given or unexpected situation. A dog is a trained animal that is chosen for the task because of his degree of intelligence. Dogs who come through the battery of tests and the extensive training time are certainly remarkably reliable in their task, but it has to be remembered that although they are able to choose between given options, changing their behaviour and responses to suit the occasion, they are none-the-less simply trained animals, and have their limitations. They work best, therefore, with people whose daily life is fairly static - those who travel the same route each day, so that the dog becomes familiar with his surroundings and alert when something changes. Then, even if the dog encounters difficulties on the way, he will at least know what the end of his journey is, and can work towards it.

A piano tuner's work is not as predictable. He may have a certain area to cover, but he will be visiting different homes all day and every day, and travelling quite widely. The dog does not have much chance to get used to his owner's route and so function with complete confidence. Given predictable situations, a dog will know what is expected of him, but taken out of his familiar sphere, he might sometimes act out of character.

I heard about a lady once who took her guide dog to London, passing through Trafalgar Square. They were proceeding nicely, when suddenly the dog made a textbook stop, and then went on. In busy London this happened often, and the lady assumed that there had been something in their way. A short time later, someone came up to her and said, "Excuse me, I hope you don't mind me mentioning it, but do you realise that your dog is carrying a pigeon?"

He had simply picked it up - still alive - as they walked! His owner was quite unaware of what had happened, but she did wonder how long her dog would have kept it, and what he would have done with it!

He would never have dreamed of doing such a thing in regular surroundings because he would be trained to follow a pattern, but in an unusual situation, his rules were somewhat blurred and his instinct came into play.

When I finally arrived at the guide dog centre in Leamington Spa, I found out that it was to be a time of assessment for me - not only the dog. Much had to be considered. First, the staff made clear to me what I would be taking on.

"You do realise, don't you, that once you have a dog its going to change your life?" I was told, firmly. "You are going to have to look after it, groom it, be responsible for feeding and making sure it does all it has to do before going out, so that there are no problems with fouling, etcetera. And in addition, you are going to be responsible for the dog when you go into people's homes as a piano tuner. Your dog will only function efficiently so long as you keep the rules too."

Clearly, it was not to be a case of simply taking on a particularly clever pet. It would be a working partnership, and would take commitment from me, too.

Then they got around to asking questions about mobility. "How do you get around now?" they asked.

"I just - go!" I said. I never had any fears about getting around, and made few allowances for obstacles - which was why I needed a dog, I thought. It reminded me of the times when I used to go home from the workshops by bus. I had to cross the road as soon as I got off the bus, then go round a corner to the left, and straight on, home. In days when buses were crewed by a conductor as well as a driver, the conductress on my route used to say "Cross him over, turn him to the left, and he'll GO!" I felt like clockwork!

I therefore had to undergo some assessment tests to find out the speed of my pace and how much anticipation I made for curbs and such like. It wasn't much - I used to charge ahead, anticipating anything and everything as I walked.

The trainer spoke seriously to me. "You will have to re-think the way you go on," he warned. "You are a fearfully independent person - you anticipate curbs and obstacles all the time...."

"I've had to," I said. "The time I didn't anticipate a lamp post, I had three stitches in my head!"

"Well, things will be different if you have a dog," the trainer continued. "Paradoxically, to gain more independence, you will have to lose a certain amount of what you have. You must give it up to the dog. Unless you are prepared to do that, you won't qualify for a dog at all."

I discovered that trusting the dog was the most difficult part. I remembered, however, that I seemed to be having more and more accidents, and that a dog would avoid all this happening. I had to be sensible and learn to trust him.

A great deal of dog psychology is used in the training of each guide dog. A system of instinct, checking and reward is used so that the dog learns that some actions bring reward, others bring a severe jerk on the harness.

He must learn, for instance, that at all costs he must stop and sit at the curb. If, therefore, he charges ahead without stopping, he feels a sharp jerk on the harness, and he is checked. As soon as he complies with the command, he is patted and praised. The whole process is concerned with disincentive versus incentive.

The trainer builds into the dog disincentive first - 'you mustn't do that or it will jerk you'. A good dog loves to be petted and praised and will willingly comply to please his owner.

A friend of mine once had a dog that insisted on running after cats - dragging her owner with her. Such a potentially dangerous situation would have to be rectified for the benefit not only of the owner, but also of the dog, and so the wayward animal went back to the training centre for correction.

She was re-trained by using mild electric shocks. Every time she went to take off after a cat, she received a small shock - not enough to harm her or even to hurt very much, but just enough to make her halt. After a time she realised that unpleasantness was associated with cats, and her behaviour changed. Now, each time she saw a cat without reacting to it, the trainer praised her profusely, and the dog responded happily. Soon she became content to forget cats and please her owner instead.

When I eventually passed my tests and was allocated Donna, a beautiful pale yellow Labrador, my trainer, Mr. Tucker, told me adamantly:

"You've got to realise that in the first month she is going to try you out. Her nature requires that she must accept you as her new pack leader. Until now, I have filled that role in her life, but I am giving way to you, and this leaves a gap which she will contest herself."

I did not realise it would all be so complicated. My trainer had not finished.

"You have not yet established yourself, and although we have begun the process, she will quite naturally make attempts to assert herself. You will have to be very firm until she realises that you are in charge."

I had been warned in this respect from the moment I came into contact with Donna. My trainer told me that as soon as he entered my room with her, I must offer her food. This would be construed in her mind as the offering of a new pack leader, and she would notice the reaction of her existing pack leader - the trainer. He would, of course, back off, effectively passing her on to me, her new leader, and Donna would begin to transfer her allegiance.

However, most dogs will take advantage of the changeover and try to assert themselves, so we watched to see what Donna would do in those first few moments of our meeting.

"She's going to be fine," said the trainer, as Donna seemed relaxed in my company. "Look - she's circling you - it's her sign of acceptance. There is no challenge in her behaviour."

I petted her genuinely. She was a beautiful, loving dog, and I knew we would be happy together. But the warning remained.

"Let her have her own way at your peril," insisted the trainer, and I determined to make sure I could be proud of Donna, and that she could be completely happy with me. She remained with me for ten years until she died, and it was to be another four or five years before I could face applying for another dog.

Andy exhibited a totally different character from Donna. Perhaps it had something to do with his being male, but he did not accept a new pack leader without putting up at least something of a fight!

We had not been together long, when one day we went for a walk at about half-past-three in the afternoon. He was fine while we walked up the avenue, but when we turned left to go towards the village, he must suddenly have thought of food. He knew that it would not be too long before we returned and he would be fed. However, we carried on for a bit until I told him, "Okay, Andy, we've walked enough," and we turned towards home. Up until that moment, his pace had been leisurely, but as soon as he turned round, it quickened.

"Steady! Steady!" I called sharply, but Andy had 'home' and 'food' firmly in mind and I could tell by his continued pace that he was not responding. The incident seemed to be minor, and to an untrained eye would probably not be worth bothering about, but I knew that no matter how insignificant, if Andy was allowed his own way in this, then he would want it in other perhaps more important matters in the future.

I could sense that I had a battle on my hands. One of us would have to come out of it the victor, and if it should be Andy, then I would have lost him for good. I needed to find a way to assert my authority over him.

When we got back to the avenue, normally I would give instruction at the curb to go right. Instead, I said, "Complete turn. We're going back to the village."

But Andy turned right.

It was already an important disobedience, so I stopped him, sat him down, and instructed him to go back to the curb. He refused.

I had now to cancel my instruction by saying 'stay' in a tone of voice that he would recognise, and begin again. In this way in the dog's mind the instruction is therefore cancelled.

"Right," I said, firmly, and gave the order to return to the curb in a much sterner voice. But Andy would not budge. This time I would have to enforce my command physically. I cancelled the instruction again, then gave it once more very firmly, but at the same time with a hard jerk on the harness. I practically lifted him of his behind! At last he obeyed.

We only went a little way, however, his pace being very slow and dejected. It seemed as though he was saying '......this is really too bad'! But when I said 'turn right' again, he did so. I steadied him, and he recovered. The crisis passed, and I had been firmly installed as his leader.

If I had not credited the incident with the importance it deserved and let him win, I would have made it very, very difficult for myself in the future, because Andy was a dominant male. It is not an easy lesson to learn. I have known people who have not managed it, and they are left with dogs that are out of control. The dog has become the leader. Then again, I have known those who are far too rigorous with their dogs - they don't trust them at all, and they both suffer.

The dog and his owner are essentially a partnership - they must trust and understand the duty they have to each other, otherwise the partnership will not work. Some people have even been prosecuted for cruelty to their dogs, and this usually arises through frustration and a lack of trust.

The problem is more acute with guide dogs because they are trained to a fine balance of leading and yet obeying, and since Alsatians have very high Intelligence Quotients, they are often the best breed to undertake the training. Labradors are also good learners, but they have a different kind of temperament which is more amenable to the kind of exploitation which makes them good guide dogs. Alsatians are more dominant, but if they can be won over, then they make the best workers. Even in humans a high IQ will render one more able to anticipate and think things through, and less likely to want to be subject to other people.

Once the owner has established himself with his dog, his worries are not entirely over because he then has to contend with the attitudes of the people he meets. Guide dogs attract attention, and most people like to give some show of affection which often includes feeding the dog some treat. This, of course, is absolutely forbidden, for to offer food is the prerogative of the pack leader. In the dog's mind, the well-meaning admirer is vying for the leadership of the pack, and usurping the position of the owner. Most people cannot know this, of course, but the blind owner must try to stop this kind of thing happening, or it can cause all kinds of problems between him and his dog.

Another reason why guide dogs should not be fed other than by their owners is because it is not good for their health and well being. A dog's natural instinct is to eat whenever food is on offer. In its primeval state, a dog would eat when it could. If it found game, it would fill up and then go and lie down, perhaps going for days without more food. In the domestic situation, lots of dogs get food as and when they want it, so will become overweight. A pet's food is readily available, and must therefore be controlled for his own good. Where guide dogs are concerned, a badly fed dog is an unhappy dog and therefore an unreliable worker.

At Leamington, the Guide Dogs for the Blind Association could have up to one hundred dogs - including puppies- under instruction at any one time, and feeding is a strictly controlled ritual. The meat is stored in huge buckets to await mealtime. I heard once that one of the buckets somehow got out of place, and was found by a determined dog. He gorged himself on the meat until he could hardly walk!

When the trainer found him very soon after, he had to act quickly. He just got hold of the dog, wrapped his arms around him and squeezed! The startled dog discovered that he could not hang on to his gargantuan meal and most of it conveniently came up! The trainer explained that the dog's digestion is very slow, and the meat came back almost unchanged! This is why a dog will only need one meal each day - or even every two days if it is a good meal. More than this will make him gain too much weight.

My dog, Andy, had one besetting sin where food was concerned. A dreadful thief, he would try to steal at every opportunity, and we needed to watch him very carefully. However, on one occasion a friend brought us a fruit and nut cake, and Margaret and I went out leaving it still in its wrapping on the kitchen table. When we returned Andy had eaten the lot. Only a small scrap of wrapping paper remained! For the next three or four days he belched walnuts!

Our reaction to his misdemeanour was to starve him, giving him only egg and milk until he had digested the stolen food. "You've had enough, you know that," I told him firmly. "You've had your full calorie intake for the next two days in one fell swoop. That's all you can have for the time being."

If I allowed him more, he would put on weight, and the Association would point this out to me when they made their regular checks. We are given strict weight parameters to adhere to, and if we fail to keep within them, the dog might be removed from our care. I used to weigh Donna and Andy regularly - usually on the railway scales which are used to weigh parcels. Donna used to sit on them as good as gold. It is possible of course, to weigh yourself, then pick up the dog and weigh together to find out how much the dog weighs, but with a fairly hefty Labrador that is not the easiest option! Then I was required to send in a report to the Association about the dog's health, social behaviour and work. The dogs were monitored very carefully, and I had no wish to spoil the record.

Throughout my years of guide dog ownership, I am afraid I must have upset quite a few well-meaning folk who thoughtlessly tried to feed my dog. I was completely misunderstood when I said: 'please do not feed him', and sometimes I even got angry. But explaining why is a complicated procedure that is impossible to begin with a stranger in the street! Ideally, people should ask first before approaching a dog at all.

Most of the time I have noticed that people will talk to my dog rather than me! There seems to be a kind of inherent embarrassment in many folk where disability is concerned, and it seems that some people tried to overcome it in my case by speaking to the dog.

I believe another reason why people will approach the dog rather than a blind owner is because sighted people rely a great deal on eye contact. They like to establish eye contact before saying anything, and whereas a guide dog owner cannot do this, the dog will - so they talk to the dog.

Now that I no longer have a dog, and at times when I am involved in evangelistic work, I often have to make a point of mentioning that if anyone wants to talk to me after the meeting, I would be happy to meet them. I add, however, 'please don't expect me to respond with a smile when you look at me. As soon as you become audible, however, you become visible in my world. Speak, and I will know you are there'.

When I was training in Leamington with Donna, I discovered that late in the training when the dog's leadership is being transferred to his new owner, the trainer lets you go out on your own with the dog, and circulates in a car so that he can see how you work together. They even have several cars to use on the route so that the dog cannot get to know it and realise that his previous leader is still around!

The trainer gave me instructions that when we got to the shops, I must sit the dog and wait for him to come to us. At the appropriate time I did what I had been taught - let down the harness so the dog would sit, thus indicating to him that I was now in the lead. While we were in this position, a lady came out of the shop and came over to us.

"Oh, you darling!" she enthused, "You darling!"

"Madam," I replied, "this is so sudden!"

"Not you - the dog!" she hastily added with a laugh.

It was the kind of thing that happened often. Playing 'second fiddle' to a dog - even ones as beautiful as Donna or Andy - does not do very much for one's self-esteem!

I used to enjoy taking my dog to meetings where he or she would sit very patiently at my feet for the whole time. Andy used to know when the benediction was said - he would often get up and stretch at this point as though he knew it would be time to go home!

Once when I was taking an assembly in a school in Northern Ireland, I played a very rhythmical arrangement of 'Go Tell it on the Mountain' A few seconds into the song, a buzz went around the hall, and they all began to laugh. I was a little disconcerted, but continued to the end of the piece. Afterwards they told me what had happened. Andy, sitting beside me, had started wagging his tail exactly in time with the music! Everyone thought that I had trained him to do that!

Sometimes I used the pack-leader theory in my talk.

I would illustrate the fact that Satan weaned the whole human race away from the original 'pack leader' in the guise of a serpent. Man willingly followed on. From that time, God continually made Himself known to his wayward creation, but they didn't understand. Similarly, my dog wants to go his own way, and it is very difficult for me to make myself understood by him. The only way I could fully be understood by a dog, would be to become a dog myself, so that we would be on the same terms. God knew that to be understood by His creation, He would have to become one of them, and so He planned drastic measures to win us back to Himself as the original 'pack leader' by becoming one of us so that we could have some understanding of Him.

I often included illustrations in my talk concerning the peril of disobedience and the pleasure of obedience, using examples of my dog's behaviour. I would suggest that Andy might take it into his own mind one day to do his own thing. If he suddenly launched us both into the road when a car was coming, we would be killed. This pictured the peril of disobedience. Then I would demonstrate the pleasure of obedience by getting Andy to stand, sit and go down, and then I'd praise him thoroughly. There would be no doubts about his pleasure when everyone saw his tail wag until it looked as though it would fall off! His eyes would glisten, and it would be obvious that he knew he had done well.

I heard a lovely story some time ago from a prominent blind broadcaster, David Scott Blackhall, who was visiting the Torch Trust for the Blind. He reckoned that his dog was so obedient and well trained that he could tell him exactly which shop to go to and the dog would go without more direction.   It didn't matter whether it was the Chemist or the Butcher, the dog only needed to hear the word and be given instructions and he would go.

One day, David told his dog to take him to the travel agent. The dog set off confidently with his master holding fast to the harness. Eventually he turned into a doorway and sat.

"Good boy," praised David, and went into the shop. At this point the dog seemed a little uneasy and David noticed. Soon an assistant came up to them.

"Can I help you, sir?" he asked in hushed tones.

"Er.........this is the travel agent, isn't it?" queried a puzzled David.

"Well, sir," answered the assistant with a grin, "it depends on where you want to go - we are the undertakers!"

CHAPTER FIVE

TUNED IN TO THE NEED

A PIANO TUNER MUST necessarily be prepared for all kinds of receptions and attitudes when he goes into people's homes. Naturally, folk are more relaxed on their own ground, and they are often more ready to chat. Children are perhaps the most endearing in this respect. They have little or no inhibitions when it comes to seeing a blind man in their home, and will react accordingly.

One little girl stood beside me for ages watching my every movement. At about nine years old, she had been learning to play the piano herself, and appeared to be greatly encouraged when she saw what I was doing. She noticed that I jabbed at the keys rather monotonously one by one and she found this very puzzling. Surely I must have been learning to play the piano far longer than she had, yet she had progressed much further than this in her short learning time!

"Mummy", she called delightedly, as she ran out of the room. "The man can only play with one finger!"

After I finished, I asked her to play for me. She sat up on the piano stool very importantly and showed me what she could do.

"That's great!" I told her. "It won't be long before you can play like me!" While she thought about that, I explained what I had been doing to the piano, and then I played for her. This time she listened avidly and we parted on the best of terms.

Another little girl of obvious school age stood by me whilst I was tuning, and I asked her why she was at home instead of being at school. "Oh well," she said proudly, "you see, I've got conjunctiveyesight!"

Children come out with the most applicable sayings sometimes. One of these came from a little boy of about eight who also stood by me, fascinated, as I tuned his mother's piano. Having watched me patiently for some time, he was even more interested when I took a sheet of paper from my case and began to make a paper boat. I finished it off with a little sail on the top, and then gave it to him.

He was obviously delighted, and ran to show his mum.

"Mummy!, Mummy! Look what the man's made me! He's blind, but he's got eyes in his fingers!"

What better way is there to describe my situation? 'Out of the mouths of babes........!'

As I went about my rounds in the Birmingham area, I did not anticipate that my knowledge of French would prove very useful. Up until then, I had classed French together with other subjects taught at school in the category of those not likely to be exactly vital to the welfare of the blind person. I had been quite good at French - musical folk very often are good at languages since they need a good ear to catch the minute inflections of the unfamiliar sounds.

It so happened that I obtained a customer who was the French wife of a Swiss ophthalmic surgeon. The lady absolutely refused to learn English for some reason, so whenever I called to tune her piano, she would greet me with 'Bonjour,' and 'entre' instead of 'come in', and instead of 'mind the step' I heard 'attention la marche'. It made my job a lot easier knowing that I could understand what she required, and that I could converse with her about the changes necessary to her piano.

However, I had no idea that my French was any better than that of anyone else until I went to advise about a tuning in Bromsgrove. The daughter of the family asked me to call, but when I phoned to arrange a time to visit, a lady answered whom I realised must be her mother, whom I had been warned could only say 'yes' and 'no' in English. It occurred to me that perhaps she should not have been answering the phone unless she expected a call from someone who spoke French, since she would be distinctly at a disadvantage - and so would her confused caller!

Gratefully I could tell her that I was the piano tuner, and I succeeded in making her understand that I wanted to call on Thursday to tune the piano for her daughter.

When I arrived there on the day, the mother wasn't there, but the daughter wanted to ask me a question.

"Mother wants to know where you learned to speak French," she asked.

"Oh dear," I answered nervously, "was it that bad?"

"Oh no," she said brightly, "on the contrary, she thought you must have studied in Paris."

Unable to grasp what I heard, I spluttered, "I've never been to Paris in my life."

The young woman was puzzled. "How have you learned such good French then?"

"Simply through a course of Linguaphone records," I answered, bemused.

"Ah, that's it, then," she chuckled. "The people who make those records are all from the Sorbonne in Paris. You have simply picked up their accents superbly well."

I had not realised when I took the trouble to work with the records in my spare time after leaving college, that it would be so useful.

Another new customer presented me with a completely different kind of problem. Just before lunch time one day, I presented myself at the customer's home and prepared, as usual, for a longish stay with an unfamiliar piano. The lady showed me into the front room, and I went forward gingerly, so as to learn the layout of the room. It was not difficult. My customer certainly had got her priorities right. The piano enjoyed sole occupancy of the room. Nothing more stood in the room at all and I soon discovered that the family had only just moved into the house. I set down my case of tools, and felt the piano to acclimatise myself with it. I noted that the top of it was open and leaning against the wall.

"Have you had your lunch?" my customer asked hospitably.

"Well, no," I answered, noticing the strong smell of cooking permeating the empty room, "but please don't worry, I shall have mine when I get home."

"Oh, you can't wait that long," she went on.. "Ours is nearly ready, I'll bring you some in."

Ignoring my protestations, she bustled out, and I started my work.

A short time later the door opened and a stronger smell of dinner wafted towards me. "Here you are," said my genial hostess. "It's 'Shepherd's Pie'. I'm sure you must be hungry."

Thanking her, I put out my hands to receive the plate.

"Can you manage it like that?" she asked. "I'm sorry we don't have a table for you to sit at." Then putting a knife and fork on the plate, she disappeared once more from the room. I thought for a minute. While I held the plate in one hand, I could not use the knife and fork together, so I put the knife on the end of the piano keyboard, and, sitting there on the piano stool, I balanced the plate on my knee and ate with the fork.

I had not quite finished the 'Shepherd's Pie' when my generous customer reappeared with a plateful of pudding.

"Here you are," she said. "This should keep you going until tea-time." But seeing that I had not quite finished the first course, she added, "Now, where shall I put it?" The only available surface in the room was the floor, so she simply placed the dish at my feet, and went out, leaving the door ajar. Seconds later, I heard a quiet 'swish' which told me that the door had opened, and the pad of feet followed by a slurping noise informed me that the family dog had enjoyed a forbidden addition to his diet.

I'm afraid I never knew what delicious delights I had missed, and neither did I let on to my hostess. But it was not until later that it occurred to me that she might have got the idea that I licked the plate clean!

A friend of mine suffered a much more disconcerting experience with a dog. Although registered blind, Cyril had a little sight. He was also a very big man, and narrowly missed falling headlong when he tripped over something as he walked up the front path of a house where he went to tune a piano. He tried to see what he had kicked, but couldn't make it out, so he dismissed it, and went in to get on with his job.

A little while later, my friend realised that something had happened.

"What's the matter?" he heard the husband ask his wife.

"It's the dog," came the tearful reply.

"What's wrong with the dog?" her husband asked anxiously.

"He's dead!" said the wife. Then added, "I found him on the front path."

With a jolt, Cyril realised what he had tripped over - but there was more to it than that. Could he have done something dreadful? Could it have been that the poor dog had been simply asleep when Cyril tripped over him, and perhaps the inadvertent kick with large, heavy boots actually.......... He couldn't bear to think of the prospect.

Cyril continued with his tuning. It would do no good to voice his doubts, but it was thereafter to be a continual source of anguish to him as to whether his clumsiness caused the death of the family's pet, sleeping peacefully in the sun on the front path, or whether he had tripped over a pet that had already died......

A traumatic experience which happened to me and which upset me a lot concerned a pet budgie. I was tuning a piano in Birmingham on a very cold day when the temperature had not risen above freezing all day. Being very small, the house had only one living room into which was crammed almost everything the family owned, including a budgie in a cage. In the grate a large fire blazed away so that the room felt oppressively warm as I came in from the cold.

Taking off my coat, I noticed that two children were talking to a budgie called Benjie who was flying about the room. He apparently flew to a mirror hanging on the wall above the fireplace and perched there. I got on with my work, and the children's mother sat soporifically in a chair beside the fire.

Some time later as I was absorbed in my tuning, Benjie must have succumbed to the heat and dozed off. Sadly, he fell from the mirror - straight into the fire. The cries from the children were pitiful.

"Benjie! Benjie!" they wept, distraught, but the little bird had been killed instantly. The mother tried to console them by saying that he would not have felt a thing, but the incident naturally caused a great deal of distress. Nearly as upset as they were I finished the piano tuning after a confused pause. It was all very difficult, and the shock and horror of the situation remained with me for a long time.

The incident made me think of the condition of so many people who are cushioned in their worlds of comfort, oblivious to the Gospel which could bring them salvation, and yet the Bible says: '...the day of the Lord will come like a thief in the night. While people are saying: 'Peace and safety," destruction will come on them suddenly.....and they will not escape.'[4] It is an illustration I have never felt able to use in a sermon, because it upsets me too much.

Another depressing story, but this time with a happier ending, concerned a lady whose address I had been given by the Birmingham Workshops for whom I worked soon after I qualified.

As soon as she opened the door I could tell that the lady was deeply troubled.

I don't quite know whether other people can 'pick up vibes' in this way, or whether my blindness has heightened my awareness, but to me, people's moods certainly seem to be immediately apparent. The woman who opened the door had more on her mind than my tuning her piano.

"Oh, it's you," she said, listlessly, "come in."

"Good morning. How are you?" I asked, but it was not quite the meaningless greeting which expects a non-committal answer.

She responded immediately. "I'm afraid I'm not very well at all," she said.

"Oh dear, I'm sorry to hear that," I said, and since she seemed to want to talk, I added, "What's the matter?"

"Well, " she began, "if I'd had enough money left in the gas meter, I wouldn't have been here to open the door to you."

Now usually, my policy has to be that when I am working, I confine my work to tuning the piano, not evangelising, and I will never mix the two unless I have clear indication that I should. This seemed to be one of those times. Very concerned, I asked her why.

"I just want to stop living," she said. "I've had enough. If the gas hadn't run out, I would have managed it by now."

"In that case," I told her as we walked into the living room, "before I tune your piano, we are both going to get on our knees and thank God that the money ran out!" It was all so dramatic! I would never usually do anything like this, but I felt sure that on this occasion I had been right. I simply asked God to reveal Himself to her, and to fill her with His peace. When I finished, the atmosphere had changed wonderfully. It felt as though refreshing dew settled in the room.

"Thank you so much!" said the lady. "I feel so much better now."

I tuned her piano, and left her in God's hands, grateful that I had arrived at the right time and that I could respond to His leading in such a difficult situation. It impressed upon me the need to be continually aware of a sense of moving in the ways of God at all times.

In a similar fashion, more recently I arrived at the home of a young lady who eventually became a member of our church. Almost as soon as I arrived, I knew I would not be tuning her piano that day. She began asking me questions immediately, and as I sat down to answer some of them, I prayed a few 'telegraph' prayers that God would be in control of my answers.

After a while, we prayed together, and she was joyfully restored to a close relationship with the Lord. She would later admit that she had not only been saved from sin, but from suicide, and that God sent me that day, not to tune her piano, but to show her the way of salvation.

Another piano I nearly didn't tune belonged to Joe and Myrtle Patterson of Northern Ireland. My trip to Ireland was for the purposes of evangelism, but I often need to finance my evangelistic work by tuning pianos - if there is no suitable tuner in the district - and the Patterson's piano happened to be on my list.

Joe Patterson and his wife had three daughters and a son, and the three girls were Christians, but also gifted musicians who sang Gospel songs together in close harmony. One of the girls asked me to tune their piano, but also mentioned that she and her sisters had been praying that I might be able to speak to their parents about Christianity at the same time.

The mother greeted me warmly, and I set to tuning the piano which was grossly out of tune, and which I could tell would take me about two hours to complete. But Mrs. Patterson wanted to chat. "I believe you know my girls go around singing at meetings," she said.

"Yes," I confirmed. "I've heard them. They are very good."

"I'm very glad they do this," went on Mrs. Patterson. "It's a wonderful thing......" and she trailed off thoughtfully.

"You are very proud of your daughters, aren't you?" I commented.

"Yes, of course," she agreed. "Any mother would be."

"You're glad that they are Christians, then?" I ventured.

"Oh yes," she said confidently.

"Well, why aren't you one too?" I added somewhat cheekily.

She thought for a moment. "I don't know," she said simply, not questioning my assumption.

"Would you like to know how to become one?" I went on, putting down my tuning lever. "I could tell you now, but I am here to tune your piano and it will take me quite a long time. Do you think you could come to the meeting I'm speaking at tonight? I will be explaining what it means to be a Christian, and I will have you especially in mind when I speak."

"That would be a good idea," she said, amenably. "I'll see if my husband will come too, and we will hear our girls sing at the same time."

I was thrilled to be told at the start of the meeting that the whole family had arrived in the hall, and afterwards both husband and wife accepted Jesus Christ as their Saviour. Later, the son told me that he couldn't sleep that night for excitement because his parents had at last become Christians. It bound the family together more closely than ever before.

I was reminded again that although I go to tune a piano, God occasionally has something greater in mind. I always have to be ready to 'tune into' that - not just the piano!

CHAPTER SIX
MOBILE GOSPEL

TO MY GREAT DELIGHT, and for just two-and-a-half years, it so happened that piano tuning slipped to a place of secondary importance in my working life. It did not last as long as I would have liked, and necessarily it happened before I married, (needless to say!) but in 1959 I accepted an invitation to join Reg and Grace Tomlinson, gospel duetists, as their pianist. They provided song ministry for campaigns and meetings in any part of the country, and travelled around living in a caravan. I travelled with them, my accommodation being a small, confined room at one end of the caravan. It was far from ideal, but we willingly coped with cramped conditions for the advantage of not having to pack and unpack suitcases, and struggle with strange beds.

During the nineteen fifties and sixties, a number of organisations took advantage of the atmosphere of the times and started large scale Evangelisation. The National Young Life Campaign (N.Y.L.C.) was one of them, with access to a number of gifted preachers who became household names. Grace, Reg and I helped them sometimes as we, too, travelled around the country. Another 'up and coming' group was the grandly named Movement for World Evangelisation, whose lofty aim was spelled out in their title.

In 1965 they asked me to help them with a Crusade in Portugal when their team pianist had to pull out for some reason or other. Margaret flew out with me and we had a wonderful time with them there, but I was both pleased and surprised when their organising officer, Ben Peake, telephoned me again some time later.

"We are hoping to put together a full-time team of evangelists and ministers who would always be available for ministry work," He told me. This would be an exciting venture, eliminating the frustrating problem of trying to find a group of people who would be able and willing to give up their holidays to take part in a crusade. A full-time team would be available at all times to go anywhere.

"We would like you to think and pray about joining us as a full time evangelist and musician," he said.

The prospect excited me, but I had already committed myself to working with the Torch Trust for the Blind, setting up 'Fellowship Centres' all over the country wherever they were needed. This work was still expanding, and it would not be possible to leave it just yet, at least.

"Do you think Torch would be in a position to support you financially?" Ben asked. I assured him that there was nò question of that. I still earned my living through piano tuning.

"Right then," he said resolutely. "Please think about joining us either full-time or part-time. We would be quite happy for you to continue your work with Torch, so long as you were available to take part in crusades for us when necessary."

So in May 1970, I became a full-time evangelist with MWE, whilst fitting in my work for Torch, and a very interesting, but frantic time in my life began.

These were exciting and wonderful days of mission, when the message of salvation was preached to many by a variety of high-profile preachers. The standard had been set by the Americans as Billy Graham began his worldwide crusades, transforming the format of the meetings with expert musicians and organisation. This kind of professionalism had not been seen in our churches or public meetings before, and we enjoyed working under such well-known evangelists as Don Summers, Marshall Shallis, Frank Farley and Roy Hessian, and as the Youth For Christ movement attracted a generation of young people to the gospel, so we joyfully gave up home comforts to work for the Lord while we had the opportunity.

Comfort may have been at a premium, but fun there was a-plenty! We would do a tour of Britain in a series of one-night stands. When someone asked 'What's the schedule for the week?' the answer might be (at a time when football reigned supreme in many towns) 'Edinburgh today, Glasgow tomorrow, Newcastle on Tuesday and Sheffield Wednesday!' We saw fun in almost everything, and teased each other unmercifully.

Once when we were in Northern Ireland for a meeting in Bangor Town Hall, someone noticed an advert on the Town Hall. He read out the message announcing our imminent arrival with the words:

'THE MEN FROM THE MOVEMENT ARE COMING...
Featuring PETER JACKSON - BLIND PAINIST'!
"Hey! That's wrong," I protested.
"Oh, no it isn't", retorted my colleagues, "it's exactly right!"

I have no idea how many churches and chapels I have visited over the years - probably thousands - but each one had its own character and problems. Once when I was to feature at George Duncan's church, 'The Tron', in Glasgow, Mr. Duncan decided to interview me in order to draw out my testimony. I understood that I would have to climb the steps of the very high, imposing pulpit from where Mr. Duncan preached. In this lofty position, the congregation would all see me clearly.

When moving about a place the usual method is for me to hold someone's arm and let him or her lead me. In this way I can easily feel the ups and downs of the path and duplicate their steps without effort. However, the spiral pulpit steps of 'The Tron' are narrow enough only for one person to walk at a time, so when my turn came to give my testimony, I was obliged to climb them following behind Mr. Duncan during the singing of the next hymn. But I had not been aware that official preaching wear for 'The Tron' consisted of a long, ankle length gown which trailed behind him on the steps as he walked.

So as I picked my way carefully up the spiral steps, I was alarmed to discover I had stepped on Mr. Duncan's gown, nearly pulling him backwards down the steps on top of me! Apologising quickly as Mr. Duncan steadied himself, I added, "Do you realise what hymn they are singing?"

He responded with a chuckle.

"Very appropriate," I went on, "Courage brother, do not stumble'!"

It is a tremendous privilege to be allowed to preach in so many different pulpits all over the country. I always try to bring to the people the message that I feel God has for them in particular, and sometimes one can preach directly into a given situation. But there are pitfalls to avoid in doing this.

Some years ago, my good friend John Blanchard inadvertently fell into a very embarrassing trap when he counselled a young lady who had asked him the way of salvation. He wanted to leave a verse with her that would give her something to remember and think about as she considered the steps she would be taking. So he gave her Proverbs chapter 11; verse 22.

After John had been home for some days he received a letter from the lady. She was clearly concerned about the verse left with her and asked him for an explanation as to why he had chosen that particular verse. She just couldn't understand what he meant by it. John looked it up quickly. It read 'As a jewel of gold in a swine's snout, so is a fair woman which is without discretion...........'!

He really meant to give her chapter 10 verse 22, which reads 'The blessing of the Lord, it maketh rich, and he addeth no sorrow with it'! The mind boggles as to what the poor girl felt as she struggled to apply it to her situation! What a good thing she had been concerned enough to write and ask for an explanation! Since then I (and no doubt, John) have been very careful about quoting verses.

Necessarily, I do have an enormous amount of Scripture stored in my memory - something that would be advisable for all sighted people to take on board. Sadly, they have such easy access to the Scriptures that memorising is not a priority. This kind of access is not open to me - especially when the Braille copy of only one book of the Bible can be a very weighty volume. It is far more convenient to me to memorise as much as possible, and this I have put into effect gladly so that I have a wealth of Scripture that I can call on at any time.

In the days of the Communist regime in Russia, the persecuted Christians made enormous efforts to memorise huge chunks of the Scriptures, simply because copies were scarce. One priceless copy of a book of the Bible would be passed secretly around the vast congregation, and each person would try to learn by heart as much of it as possible in the brief time that it was available to them. It always makes me wonder what would happen to us here in Britain if persecution should come and all our copies of the Bible were banned.

Here we are, with probably several copies in each household, and yet the majority of people have little or no Scripture committed to memory. We might then discover just how barren our lives are without God's Word to refer to. For my part, it is, of course, quite impossible for me to do what other ministers of the Word can do. For instance, I cannot carry the whole Bible with me on tour, or even for weekends. I have to copy out likely passages that I might use, with the barest of notes, and at first, all this had to be done by hand. Now, of course, with my computer and Braille printer things are so much easier. But even in my on-the-spot preparation in someone's home, I can't just take a Bible in my hands. God undertakes, however, and aids my memory.

John Blanchard always put every bit of himself into whatever he did. He was the kind of man who moved with conviction, and when he moved, he acted heartily and with all his might.

At one time he became involved in physical exercise in a big way. He decided that it was a key to health and that he would not neglect his daily routine of exercises, come what may. This could have had dire consequences years later during the time I worked with MWE. We happened to be staying in a cottage in the North-west.

On the first morning, Peter Smith (who joined us as soloist) and I followed the delicious aroma of bacon and eggs wafting up from the kitchen, and presented ourselves in the dining room without delay. John was nowhere to be seen.

The rooms of the cottage were quaint and small, but cosy; the ceilings low and with a light hanging down over the dining table. We settled ourselves to eagerly await the bacon and eggs.

"When is Mr. Blanchard coming down?" asked our hostess.

"He'll be down shortly," I answered, hoping she did not intend to put off serving the breakfast until he made an appearance.

"Oh well......." She began, and then stopped. In the uneasy silence, I realised something was wrong.

"It's the light over the table," explained Peter. "It's swaying."

A moment or two later there were gasps as they noticed that the ceiling itself was bowing and bending alarmingly, with tremendous 'thumps' reverberating around the little cottage.

"Oh, my goodness!" cried our hostess.

It was all an example of the way John would throw himself into everything he did, taking Ecclesiastes 9; 10 to heart: 'Whatever your hand finds to do, do it with all your might'.........What a lot could be achieved in the Lord's service if every Christian had a similar attitude.

Marshall Shallis was another great man of God. As the leader of The Evangelisation Society (TES) at the time, he showed an enthusiasm for God in a different way. I often wondered what would have become of him if he had not come to know the Lord as his Saviour, since he possessed a legendary melancholic temperament. It seemed as though nothing ever went right for him as he saw only the pessimistic side of the situation. He was the proverbial finder of the half-empty mug, when the optimist would declare it to be half full!

We might be having a wonderful time of blessing with people coming to know the Lord through his inspired preaching, but it would never be enough for Marshall. In our conversations about him, the stories would become somewhat inflated and affected: for instance, it was said that, on the first night of a crusade, it was typical of him to agonise in prayer, beseeching the Almighty with desperate words: 'Lord, it's time for you to awake. You know that only five ministers, two deacons and thirty-seven others have been saved so far in this crusade..........'

One day he was at a certain church in Croydon, Surrey and counselled three people for salvation after he had preached. He just got outside the church when the treasurer came running up to him, and put an envelope in his hand.

"There you are, Mr. Shallis," he said, "this is for your expenses."

Marshall opened the envelope straight away and out fell 4/6d - about 23p in today's currency. Looking toward heaven, he exclaimed, "Ah, well, Lord, every little helps - at that rate it's 1/6d per soul!"

Don Summers, however, always used to say that the first convert in any of his crusades in which I was involved was the piano! He reckoned it needed the ministry of laying on of hands before it could be pressed into the service of the King! He was right in that I invariably had to spend a long time tuning the piano at any new place - sometimes even repairing it before it became half- usable. Only a rare church or organisation saw to it that their piano remained in good condition.

More often than not, the piano would be the last thing on their minds. I can still never quite understand this attitude because a good sounding piano makes such a difference to the worship and it certainly makes a great deal of difference to me!

I cannot play my best on an out-of tune, broken instrument. I need to feel it responding eagerly under my fingers - reacting to my touch as though it had been waiting to be brought to life. Then I can lead the worship effectively - responding to the moods and needs of the congregation in mutual pleasure of the worship.

To me, it is a tragedy that so many pianos are forgotten instruments - often given to the church because their owners can't get rid of them any other way.

There is another side to this story, of course. That is the one where pianos are donated to a church in memory of a loved one. It may be very much appreciated to begin with, but every piano - like the loved one - has its life span, and sooner or later it has to be buried. But how do you bury a piano that has been donated in permanent memory of someone? It's like eradicating the memory of the person, and will cause offence to the remaining relatives and acute embarrassment to everyone else.

I, therefore, am not in favour of this kind of donation, but if it has to be done, then perhaps the church should find out the rough length of life the piano has left, and with as much sensitivity as possible, notify the donor before accepting the gift unconditionally (no strings attached!) no matter how kindly it has been offered. I have come across many difficult situations caused through generously donated gifts - of all kinds - that cannot be relinquished when the life of the gift is over.

All too often, I have been invited to a church leader's home, having wrestled with a deficient piano during the Sunday services. Ostensibly the invitation is to supper, but even before the meal appears on the table, I am invited - nay almost commanded, to play their beautiful, new piano. I instinctively compare it with what the Lord has to put up with. He so often gets second best, and yet when Noah came out of the ark with his family, he made a sacrifice to the Lord of that which was perfect and clean, not wounded, ill-favoured animals.

Frank Farley was another powerful evangelist with whom I worked and whom I greatly respected. I felt sad when I heard that after a long illness he had gone to be with the Lord. When I knew him best, he was a bundle of effervescent energy, and had a gift with words.

He could transport his congregation with his wonderful descriptions and tremendous word power. He could take a joke, and we constantly pulled his leg. Bearing in mind his way with words, we would never let him forget the rare occasions when words failed him.

One day he was describing a girl on a beautiful sunny morning:

"There she stood in the centre of the room," he enthused in his delightful West country accent, his voice hushed with awe and his hands caressing the air in gestures of wonder, "relaxed and beautiful in the morning light, a gentle smile hovering around the corners of her delicate mouth and an almost imperceptible sparkle in the subtle blue of her eyes," here he paused and took a deep, wondering breath, "and then.......and then............." - his hands held motionless in the air as he sought for adequate words - "through the window behind her, the sun rose above the trees, and as though to emphasise the beauty of the moment....... It sent a shaft of vivid sunlight shining through her.........her............. head!"

His audience, carried along by the poetry of his description, crashed with a jolt. He had meant to say 'hair' of course, so instead of a sigh of agreement, he got a blank look of surprise from his listeners.

We brought the incident up at every possible occasion thereafter - especially when Frank seemed to be going 'over the top' in his descriptions!

Roy Hessian - another great man who has gone to be with the Lord, was a completely different character, but just as effective in his ministry. He used to say that there should be no striving in the Christian life. He favoured a passive approach, backed up by the picture of Christ as the Door. 'We don't have to climb to reach Jesus,' he would say, 'he is at street level. We just cross the threshold.' Then with a gentle gesture he would continue, 'and so it should be with everything we do for him - no struggle - just acknowledge him in all you do, and let him lead you gently.'

He was held in great respect, and when I realised that he would be leading our devotions in the team meetings during our Doncaster crusade, I looked forward to them eagerly. I was interested to experience not only his ministry of the Word, but also his ministry of prayer, because I usually find that men of the Word are men of prayer as well. The very first morning we got together, one or two of us prayed, then after quite a bit of quietness, Roy began to pray, and I learned a lesson. I expected to be carried within the veil to the very throne of God by this man's prayers - lifted in the eloquence and beauty of exquisitely chosen language, because I thought that all men of God were gifted in this way. But when Roy began to pray I got a shock. He simply said, "Lord, I have to admit to you that I'm terribly, terribly 'dry' this morning. I don't feel a thing and I come to you in this condition - empty, dry and withered up, but I know that you can refresh my spirit."

I could hardly believe that such a man, whose life was spent in closeness to the Lord, who had witnessed the Ruanda revival, and who was able to inspire others to similar closeness, could possibly ever feel 'dry', 'empty' or 'withered'. I was utterly amazed!

At the end of the prayer we were lifted, but the lesson I learned was that we must be honest in prayer. We can't switch on religious feelings, and anyway, God doesn't want us to feel religious in order to pray. We simply need to be honest in our praying and tell God exactly how we feel. He knows, but it helps us to tell him.

Jack Ward was another man whose ministry took me by surprise. Many will remember him as the pianist mainly for the National Young Life Campaign, and whose lively style of playing was the answer, in the fifties and early sixties, to the American professionalism.

Now and again our paths crossed and we were able to get together in ministry. When the two of us let ourselves 'go' - four hands on an unsuspecting piano, the result would be some very lively music indeed! The people loved it and delightedly used to shout for more!

However, to those who did not know him very well, Jack presented a very different image. To begin with he smoked very heavily, and this set him apart somewhat from the rest of the team. But he also found it very difficult to radiate what was obviously in his heart and so sometimes presented a strained or even sulky image. All this meant that he was often misunderstood.

This came across clearly on the first night of a crusade in Guernsey at a time before Jack had become known to the whole team. He was actually on holiday on this occasion, but he used to breeze in to join with us for the evening meetings.

Each morning we would have a team meeting when items for prayer would be offered, bearing in mind the crusade meeting of the evening before. At the first of these team meetings, Reg Tomlinson wanted to mention an item for prayer.

"I'd like to pray for a man I saw in the congregation last night," said Reg. "If ever I saw a man under conviction of sin, it was him," he went on. "I noticed he is a heavy smoker, and he looked so strained that I felt a real burden for him."

"Oh," said Ray Castro, the leader for us that morning. "Where was he sitting?"

"At the front on the right hand side looking from the platform," explained Reg. "You must have noticed him."

A questioning silence fell on the group. "Er.......was it the same man who stood to one side of the door as everyone went out?" asked Ray, tentatively.

"Yes, that's right," Reg nodded eagerly.

"Ah," said Ray, "well, that was Jack Ward!"

Reg had never seen Jack before, and he and Grace found it very difficult to come to terms with this complicated character. They had sung many of his compositions which were very popular at the time, and they, like most other people, would have had an image in their minds of the thoroughly spiritual, joyful composer who delighted many with his work. The dour, seemingly troubled personality presenting himself in reality, was anathema to them.

But Jack did have a lighter side. He had us all in stitches one morning when he came puffing in late for our team meeting. We had all wondered what had happened to him when he failed to turn up on time, and it was a full half-hour before he showed up. By that time we had had the Bible reading and the comments following it, and were well into the de-briefing session from the night before.

"Sorry I'm late," he puffed, falling into a chair.

"What on earth happened?" asked the worried leader for the day.

"Well, it was my landlady.....," began Jack, lighting up a ciga-rette. "Breakfast is supposed to be at nine, so I waited in my room as usual for her to call 'Breakfast is ready, Mr. Ward,' but it didn't happen. Then about half-past-nine I began to smell the bacon cook-ing, and it wasn't until twenty-to-ten that the call came. I hurried downstairs, and got straight on with the bacon and eggs, leaving the cereal because I knew I'd be late for the meeting. A few minutes later my landlady came in with toast and marmalade, and she said, 'I'm ever so sorry that breakfast was delayed, but I had to wait because the cat had her kittens in the frying pan!'

We often felt very vulnerable when we stayed with strange people and in strange beds. There is a sense in which one is at the mercy of one's hosts. We never know what kind of bed we will have or what kind of food we will be offered, and sometimes, what kind of atmosphere we will have to suffer.

One such time I found rather embarrassing concerned a couple with whom I stayed who were obviously experiencing tension in their marriage. The husband had a way of continually repressing his wife with scarcely veiled jokes.

"It's a good job you've come this weekend," he would jibe to me, "or I would have starved!"

Then when we came to the cakes, he would offer them, saying, "Have a 'Garden of Eden' cake."

"Garden of Eden? Why are they called that?" I asked, playing right into his hands.

With a grin of satisfaction, he gleefully told us, "Because when you've 'ad 'em - you 'eave!"

The wife had heard it all before many times, and I could tell by the tension in the atmosphere, that the continual barrage of jokes at her expense was wearing very thin.

Grace and Reg had a problem once when they were on holiday in the Lake District. They didn't have enough bed covers and were very cold. So in desperation, they took the rug off the floor and draped it on top of them. In the morning, the landlady walked in with a tray of tea!

This was the kind of pitfall we avoided by having the caravan as we travelled around. It may have been small, but at least we could keep warm and could relax completely once we had shut the door!

There was another occasion when Jack Ward became the focus of long-continued mirth during the time he played the piano for a crusade in Western-Super-Mare, Somerset.

The team had had a day off, except for a meeting in the evening, and as the weather had improved after a period of rain, Jack decided to take advantage of the sun and have a time of relaxation on the beach. He had a swim, then settled himself down on the beach, which at Western-Super-Mare is well known for having a thin layer of sand over mud.

He was very tired and soon fell asleep, only to wake up again at five to seven in the evening. To his horror, he remembered that he had to be at the meeting which started at seven. Looking down at himself, he realised that in the time he had been lying on the beach, the tide had come in and gone out, transforming the sand as it went to a sea of mud.

His back, from his neck to his heels, was now completely caked in mud, all brown and stiff round the edges where the sun had dried it. He would need a bath to remove it all. There was no time for that, though. Frank Farley would be nearly frantic by now, wondering what on earth they were going to do without a pianist. There was no more Jack could do but to simply grab his clothes, struggle into them, mud and all, and rush on to the meeting. Frank was, indeed, frantic, by the time Jack puffed into the meeting. "Jack!" he exclaimed with relief, "Get to that piano, man, quick!"

So Jack went to the piano without time to think much about the uncomfortable crackling brown mud flaking beneath his clothes, and Frank, who, of course, knew nothing about what had happened, announced the first chorus.

"Now our pianist has arrived, let's begin by singing chorus number twenty-four," he began. "Out of the Mud and the Mire"!

It did not take long for Jack's expert playing to become popular and much requested on record. His style was lively and very modern - a world away from the austere harmonies of a few years before. The Christian expression of worship had moved light years away from the pre-war seriousness, and Jack became one of the pianists who expressed the new way best.

As a young man, I loved playing duets with him on the occasional times we were together, and to hear how his playing became the expression of his Christian experience where his normally forbidding appearance would hide it.

They were wonderful days of service. What a privilege for me - a young man comparatively new to the Christian faith - to spend several years in full time service under the ministry of such men of God. I estimate that the time was probably the equivalent of an entire course of full time Bible college training. I have preached and ministered in music at many meetings over the years, but I continually thank God for the time of concentrated study he gave me as I travelled around with Reg and Grace. My living quarters in the minute corner of Grace and Reg's caravan may not have been very luxurious, but I will never know - until I get to Glory - just how luxurious was my education in the Lord which equipped me for life in that mansion in the sky!

CHAPTER SEVEN

FILEY

ONE OF THE HIGHLIGHTS of my years with MWE was the annual convention at Filey.

In the 1950's, a new kind of holiday hit the nation. Billy Butlin had the idea of setting up cheap, chalet-style accommodation in one large complex that would also include restaurants and a variety of amusements. In this way, he could provide for the total needs of whole families on holiday, avoiding the necessity of them having to go outside the camp to spend their money. Before long he had holiday camps all over the country, and it seemed as though everyone went to 'Butlin's' at one time or another.

Christian organisations took up the idea, too, and many a 'house-party' provided fellowship and light-hearted entertainment under one roof and for an all-inclusive payment.

MWE thought big, however. With people eager to share the 'holiday camp' experience, and the general atmosphere of hope and Evangelisation in the country after the war years, they approached Butlins with the proposition of hiring the entire camp at Filey for one week in September each year when the holiday season usually began to slacken off. It suited Butlins to secure the income of the camp on a regular basis, and so the Filey Convention was born. But the holiday would not be one long round of pleasure seeking. It would cater for Christians who wanted to learn and have fellowship with folk from all over the British Isles. There would be meetings with speakers who would inspire and enthuse; times of worship and prayer, and gatherings to study God's Word. The idea was that each Christian would return home revitalised to continue their daily work.

I joined the team of musicians during the heyday of the Filey Convention in 1970 and recognised its uniqueness immediately. Perhaps its secret lay in the vast numbers of Christians - five to seven thousand, plus day visitors - who came to spend a week in study and worship, or perhaps it was the tremendous sense of building fellowship amongst them. Whatever the reason, Filey could be matched no-where else. Only at the Billy Graham Rallies in the 50's had people gathered together in larger numbers to hear the Gospel, and then they would attend for only one meeting, but at Filey, thousands came to spend a whole week with God, and the atmosphere was electric.

From the Saturday when the people arrived, there was a feeling of excitement and anticipation. It all began when they made their way to the reception area to book in and receive the special folder that was the guide to the week. They would greet each other and joyfully meet up with those they hadn't seen since last year or even the year before, catching up on past news and excitedly chatting about what they would do during the week as they scanned their folders and commented on points which attracted their attention.

The folder contained information about all that would happen that week. One enclosure to which everyone eagerly looked forward was the Filey SongBook - specially compiled each year with new songs composed specifically for the week amongst old favourites. These song books would be retained and taken home at the end of the week, when the new songs would be enthusiastically introduced to the home churches - thus hopefully, bringing a taste of Filey to those unable to go, and probably prolonging the holiday in a small way for those who had gone!

Also in the folder were the notes on the whole programme, including the list of speakers with a brief outline of their life and work and details of who would be doing what and where. There would always at this time be a buzz of excited conversation as the people studied the programme and made decisions about what they wanted to do for the week. Then they would go off to their chalet or flat to unpack and prepare for the opening meeting.

Meetings took place in three different venues: The Gaiety Theatre held about three thousand people, with two other halls - The Viennese Ballroom, The Beachcomber - or similar large halls, holding between one thousand and fifteen hundred each. Several meetings ran at once during the day so the people could be diffused throughout the venues, but in the evening most people wanted to go to the Convention meeting, and then after it, there would be a large crowd for the Late Night Extra. Finding a seat, therefore, became a permanent problem. The determined solved it by preparing a flask for themselves during the day and going straight from the convention meeting to the Late Night Extra instead of going for the provided coffee and biscuits! The rest had to be content with closed circuit television, which in itself was an innovation in those days.

The Convention meetings were the most popular when we were privileged to hear some of the greatest Bible expositors of the day. Some were already well known, but others became well known partly as a result of their ministry at Filey. Their names still echo through the years: Alan Redpath, Sidlow Baxter, Stephen Olford, David Watson, Ron Dunn from the USA, and George Duncan, to name but a few. They were wonderful men of learning, but they had an additional quality that became apparent when one got to know them during the holiday week: their humanity.

An inevitable result of being set above everyone else on a platform was that the team - speakers and musicians - would appear remote from the people. Filey helped to balance this by seating us around the tables with the people for meals. We would rotate round the tables from meal to meal so that as many as possible could meet us. It was here that these great men were vulnerable. If they had a tendency to superiority, then they would be found out amongst the people, but this did not happen. They all seemed to have that elusive quality which the famous would do well to seek after: that of being confident in the execution of their gift, yet with a profound respect toward others. In return, they gained the respect of the people, and a 'Filey Speaker' became synonymous with excellence - and they still have that reputation to this day.

However, getting to know so many people had its problems.

Our days were quite full with seminars and meetings of all sorts, and it was necessary to move through the campus from place to place as we went from one meeting to another. But everyone else would be doing the same thing, so it became impossible to get straight to where you were going. Before you had gone ten yards, someone would stop you and want to talk. If you stopped to chat, you would never get to your destination, so one had to balance politeness with firmness.

"I'm awfully sorry," I would say, "I'm off to a meeting." This became our standard phrase, although some people were inevitably hurt because you could not stop and talk to them. We had no choice, though. In situations like this most people think that they have something special to say that 'won't take a moment', but the 'moments' all add up when one is tied to a timetable!

I had an additional problem with those who liked to tease me by saying, "Who is it, then? Do you remember me? I was here last year." I have a pretty good memory, but when one meets thousands and thousands of people from year to year, it becomes very difficult to pluck out just one with no other clues but their voice! I remember one lady from Sunderland who did this one year, and she added, "You must remember me - you had tea at our house fifteen years ago. Don't you remember? - You had a boiled egg!"

Nowadays, I find that often someone will come up to me and say, "I remember you from Filey." It drew people from all over the country and from every age range. Only recently I talked to a man who was married with children, and he said, "I remember you coming to the children's meeting at Filey when I was a young lad...." He still remembered. How humbling it is when people remember one's ministry for so long - and it is not only Filey that draws remembrances. It is wonderful to hear how God has blessed in particular ways and at particular times.

Another time in Belfast a lady in her mid-twenties and married with two children, came up to me and said, "I just want you to know that you came to our school when I was a fifth-former, twelve years ago, and what you said that day started me on my pilgrimage. Now I've come to faith in Christ."

This kind of thing happens all the time and it fills me with a joy which comes from the satisfaction of knowing that I was, and still am in the Lord's will.

Most of the seminars and meetings at Filey provided intensive teaching which would give the people much to think about during the weeks and months to follow, but the Late Night Extras were the times when we could 'let our hair down'. They were a light-hearted mix of humour and holiness. These were the times when the jokes would fly........

'The lady driver's car broke down, so she called out the AA.

The AA man arrived after an hour, and said, "Your battery's flat."

"Oh, dear," said the lady, "what shape should it be?"

She broke down again some time later, and the same AA man came out to her. "All you need is a bit of choke," he said.

"Where's that?" the lady asked.

"It's the knob your handbag's hanging on," said the AA man.

Yet again she broke down, and once more the same AA man went out to help. By now he was getting rather fed up. "Look here, madam," he said, "I'm afraid your car is suffering from thrombosis."

The lady was puzzled. "Cars don't suffer from thrombosis," she said.

"This one does," replied the frustrated AA man, "it's suffering from a clot behind the wheel!"

Another Late Night Extra joke went like this: A young man who had been appointed an assistant minister was to preach his first sermon. He was very nervous, but afterwards he felt he had done quite well, so in the vestry he fished for a compliment or two from his pastor. "People seem to be quite pleased....." he prompted. The pastor told him that he had done well, but did not comment further.   The young man tried again.

"There is one thing that troubles me.."

"What's that?" asked the pastor.

"When I was shaking hands afterwards, one chap went out saying, 'Oh, you're hopeless , you are......', and then he came back in and said, 'You'll have to do better next time.'"

The pastor frowned. "Was this man in a grey raincoat, and did he have rather long hair?"

"Yes, that's him," said the young minister.

"Oh," said the pastor, dismissively. "Don't take any notice of him - he only repeats what other people are saying."

Filey had this tremendous sense of humour running through it. It contrasted with other great conventions like Keswick, which tended to be rather more serious. The success of Keswick can be judged by the fact that it has been running for well over a hundred years! I attended the centenary celebrations, and made a remark that was published in the centenary magazine: I said that Keswick seemed to be all meat and no gravy! It may be so, but what a wonderful thing it is that so many people are prepared to go year after year to find the 'meat' of the Scriptures. Maybe there is hope for our country yet!

There was only one aspect of Filey which troubled me a little - in fact it did not only happen at Filey - and I found it to be an inevitable consequence of being blind. I became something of a novelty. This is the disappointing aspect of my condition, since to me, it is quite normal.   I am exactly the same as anyone else, except for the fact that I can't see - and maybe that I can play the piano reasonably well. The question will always remain as to whether I would have been able to play as well if I had never lost my sight, but it has all been part of the Lord's plan for my life, and I wouldn't have things any other way.

I do not enjoy the wondering notoriety which blindness draws in many people who see me rarely. I much prefer to be accepted as normal in the same way as do my friends who know me well. I have discovered that when a new acquaintance speaks to me, they struggle to omit words like 'see' and 'look'. It causes them acute embarrassment, of course! My friends will quite happily say, 'Did you see that programme on television the other night....' and this is of no problem to me at all.

Television doesn't have much interest for me, naturally - radio is my favourite, but my family watch television and I share with them often. I simply don't see the pictures, that's all. I can discuss it, though, because blindness, to me, is quite normal! People have no need to feel embarrassed that they might say the wrong thing! I am more bothered by the fact that they feel the need to choose their words!

But people will always be overawed to some extent by disability in others because they are unsure how to handle it. I had to overcome this by accepting the fact that it shows people are interested. It is what I am that draws their attention, and I had to learn to sustain that interest by what I do. Sighted people do not attract attention by what they are - they have to do something to engage interest in the first place. I don't have to do that. People are interested straight away because I am blind. It really helps to gain a rapport, and that gives me a platform on which to build.

Sometimes the reaction is sympathy, and this is not necessarily a bad thing. I can use this emotion, too, as a bridge builder to draw people towards the Lord, but sympathy must never be exploited. I found this out one day when I went on door to door work for Shirley

Pioneer Church where I was co-pastor with Geoff Bowater, the father of the song writer, Chris.

I knocked on a door, and a man opened it. He looked at me and realised I was blind. Immediately, he said, 'I know why you've come. You think you can prey on my sympathy and attract me to your church. Well, I'm just not interested.' And he banged the door shut. I was aghast. It hadn't occurred to me that people would misinterpret my intentions. Consequently, I have since been very loath to do door-to-door work. It gives the wrong signal.

However, handled properly, my blindness can prove of benefit. I only have to hear my announcer say 'Our visitor this morning is blind,' and a little gasp is heard rippling through the audience. My reaction is, 'Great! Now I've got their interest.'

This was true of Filey - and here we were talking to thousands of people together. I found myself rising to the challenge. But there were also characters who attracted instant attention by some other unusual feature.........

My wife, Margaret was with me, as usual, on one of the opening nights at Filey, and we were welcomed to the team prayer meeting that always took place before the main Convention meeting. During these times one could hear great men with cultured, modulated voices and skill in prayer - men like George Duncan, David Watson and others. The prayer time began, and one could not fail to be impressed by the clarity of their diction, and the flow of their well-chosen words. I used to love to hear them, and resolved to learn from their ability.

On this particular occasion, however, our minds were jerked to attention by the sound we heard. From the platform came the immortal words:

"Well, 'ow d'yer do, Lord? We're so glad we've got 'ere tergevver, but we wanna make sure yor wiv us, 'cos if you aint, we don't stand no chance!"

It was, of course, Fred Lemon, the Cockney who had been converted from a life of crime not so long before. Margaret gave me a nudge, and we had to grin. It was so incongruous, yet so natural and endearing.

A similar thing occurred at a Pentecostal Church in London. A man gave a word of prophecy - but not with the usual 'spiritual language' which runs on Authorised Version lines such as: 'Thus saith the Lord.....' No, this man attracted the attention of the congregation with: 'Arf a mo'! 'Arf a mo'!' and then went on to give his prophesy in equally vernacular fashion!

How refreshing it was! These men spoke to the Lord in the way that one would speak to a close friend - as indeed, he should be. Some people speak to the Lord as though he is a particularly critical head master, who would disregard any prayer not couched in the appropriate ecclesiastical language. It could be that many new Christians are put off praying aloud because they have not been Christians long enough to learn 'the language of prayer'. How sad this is! We should be encouraging people to talk to God as they talk to a highly respected friend. They should not have to learn a language to pray.

During the war years, a new convert came to a prayer meeting one evening. It was the kind of meeting where someone would just start up a chorus, and the pianist would follow. He thought to himself, 'This is wonderful! I wish I could start up a chorus like that, but I don't know very many.'

Anyway, suddenly he got his chance when, at the end of a prayer came the words, 'So, Lord, we pray that you will bless them all........' Immediately, he started up with 'Bless 'em all, bless 'em all........ The long and the short and the tall...........'!

In similar vein, I heard the following story from someone on the Shankhill Road in Belfast:

An organist always played very loudly after the service. He was a brilliant organist, playing Bach preludes and fugues; toccatas and all the rest, and he seemed to use the after-church time as his moment to shine. The trouble was that the congregation couldn't talk to each other for the noise of the organ. The minister got worried because he didn't want to upset the organist, but on the other hand he had to admit that the recitals shattered the atmosphere after a thought-provoking sermon.

So he invited the organist for coffee. He said, 'I recognise that you are a splendid musician, and how fortunate we are to have you as our organist, but I wonder whether in future you could play something in keeping with the message I preach - something that would carry it over in the people's minds'.

The organist said he would give this some thought. The next Sunday the minister preached about Lot's wife, and afterwards the organist launched into appropriate music. From the organ loft wafted the strains of 'The Girl I Left Behind Me'!

But the wonderful days of Filey came, like all good things, eventually to an end. Some would say that the beginning of the end occurred at the death of Lindsay Glegg. Filey had been Lindsay

Glegg's vision, and although far from young when it all began, he continued to take a part throughout its quarter-century run until the early 1980's when he was in his nineties.

One of his duties which became something of a beloved ritual to the people was his benediction after the Late Night Extra. It had become a custom to sing 'The Lord's Prayer' and then for Lindsay to step forward and pronounce the benediction in his tremulous, but distinctive voice. A simple act, but over the years it became a vital, looked forward to part of the proceedings, and most people declared that it rounded off the evening and left one feeling that it had been a wonderful night.

Then the day inevitably came when Lindsay went to be with the Lord. Questions were asked straight away as to whether Filey should end at that point. It seemed strange to imagine the week without him. But the people were still coming; its popularity had not diminished, so the final decision was that it should continue.

It never really seemed the same, however, and the writing finally appeared on the wall when Butlin's management began to say that it was not really worth their while to remain open for that September week. Perhaps it had something to do with the decline of holiday camps in the face of the rise of package holidays abroad, but they became loathe to let the camp to a crowd who did not even help to recoup losses by buying drinks at the bars. The usual holiday visitors would heap profit upon Butlins' through the sales of alcoholic drinks, but when the Christians got together, they did not need much else beside themselves.

Finally, Butlin's reported that they were selling the Filey camp, and MWE were obliged to make a decision.

There was a brief attempt to continue the wonderful times at another camp at Skegness, but this meant that the Convention could no longer be called 'Filey' - the name which had long been synonymous with this particular week. 'Filey at Skegness' was tried, and then 'New Horizons', but the atmosphere was never the same, and after a couple of years, it all had to stop. There were others who tried a similar formula for Christian conventions through the 'Dales' and 'Downs' weeks, but nothing really lasted for long until 'Spring Harvest'.

'Spring Harvest' has certainly been successful, but its ethos is quite different from the old Filey days, and draws a different crowd. Perhaps it has something to do with fashions, but as far as the music is concerned, it consists mainly of group worship, and does not include soloists of the kind who used to enrich Filey. The Filey scene in part consisted of superb musicians who lifted and focused the worship with their singing, but it seems that times have changed, and so have fashions in music, and they are rarely seen any more.

With the closing of the main Filey Convention Week, the longing to continue the good days led to a series of reunions in different parts of the country.

At one such reunion, Dave Pope and Bob Christy were leaders. Dave had masses of thick hair, but Bob was decidedly thin on top.

"It's nice to see you," said Bob to Dave from the platform.

"It's nice to see you too," responded Dave.

"D'you know......" Bob continued, "as I was coming to this reunion tonight, I thought of a very appropriate Scripture for the two of us."

"Really? What was that, Bob?"

Bob put his hand on Dave's crop of healthy hair, and then on his own shiny pate. "The Lord has given, and the Lord has taken away. Blessed be the same of the Lord!"

Perhaps that applies to Filey, too...........

CHAPTER EIGHT

MUSIC TO TRAVEL WITH

I STARTED MAKING RECORDS seriously round about 1970. I had made a couple before that, but only with essentially amateur, albeit, very competent technicians. There were a few small companies making Christian recordings; I was happy to swell the ranks of the musicians recording their talents for posterity on 33 rpm long-playing black discs. The twelve-inch records were the very latest in technology at the time.

When Bill Hamilton of Word Records approached me about making records for them, I said to Bill, "Would you really care to risk a disc?"

He replied, "We'll risk it."

So my recording career began. It was wonderful to have been asked, and would have seemed even more wonderful had I realised the precarious state of Word's finances at the time.

In retrospect, it was a step of faith on Bill's part, and amazingly enough, the series of Instant Piano began to sell really well. In order to be somewhat innovative too, I played duets with myself by means of what's known as double tracking. It was not entirely successful, and - looking back now the technicians responsible would probably disown the attempt! The Instant Piano series was followed by New Moods - a disc made specifically with coffee-bar evangelism in mind. New Moods featured the pieces I had   composed for our two boys, Timothy Fraser and Christopher. That was followed by In Concert, Just as I am and Family Favourites 1 and 2. I had intended to make one album of Family Favourites. Mr. Hamilton had booked a whole day in the studio, but by lunchtime, I had completed the record.

"What are we going to do?" asked my producer: "I've booked the studio for this afternoon as well. Do you think you could record for another disc?"

I said: "If you pray, I'll play!" Thus Family Favourites 2 came into being. (I later learned that, strictly speaking, it was against the Musicians' Union rules to produce two records at one studio booking.)

After this spate of record making in the seventies, I ceased recording for some considerable time. Word were no longer interested in recording me. Bill Hamilton had retired, and Word U.K. had become Waco: Word America Company.

American artists with sophisticated backing now dominated the Christian recording scene, and my kind of music was totally out of vogue. My kind of playing caters for a more 'mature' age-range, and most commercial recording markets have, until now, been geared mainly to young people. This may have been sensible business practice once - bearing in mind the fact that the young people of recent years have dominated popular culture and have had the finances to buy records. But today's population is becoming proportionately older and older, and it may not still be the case that the young have all the resources.

Bearing all this in mind, I resumed my recording career in the late 1980's with two Piano Praise cassettes of contemporary Christian music. I wasn't travelling quite as much then, but the distribution of these cassettes was really encouraging. The Piano had not, after all, lost its popularity. I felt humbled to realise that God was still pleased to bless the gift he had given me.

In 1992, I made He Rescued Me, a recording some of my own compositions. This was produced in Northern Ireland to celebrate twenty-one years of ministry in the province.

By now, I had begun to travel much more; consequently the distribution increased even more than had the Piano Praise cassettes. Then came Classical Gospel, which is probably the most popular recording that I have ever made. Perhaps many of my readers will know that these are classical arrangements of well-known, well-loved gospel hymns.

On 31st March 1995 I flew to Northern Ireland for yet another series of meetings. I was conscious of the growing tension between my work as a piano-tuner and the increasing tours I was undertaking. I was wondering just how long I could keep on living what I was beginning to call my 'double life'.

The following week, on April 7th, to be precise, the idea was born that was to result in Keynote Ministries. Not many months before, a minister in Cardiff had said to me, "You ought to be fully committed to your ministry."

I asked, "How?"

He replied, "Tell the churches."

The plan was that Margaret and I would produce a letter, introducing Christians to our ministry. There would be a sponsorship arrangement of a maximum of £10.00 per annum. I felt that, with all the Christians nation wide that were aware of my ministry going back many years, that there would be no problem in getting all the support we needed within twelve months. A thousand sponsors would do the trick!

Also, my original idea was to set up a Trust, and I had actually produced a Trust deed. However, when I sent it to my friends in Northern Ireland for their perusal and opinion, I was advised to keep everything under our control, rather than under the more cumbersome control of Trustees. It wasn't to be a Trust, an organisation, or even a company, just an account that would support Margaret and me in our ministry. We produced our introductory letter, introducing the sponsorship plan that we felt was singularly undemanding. We had some response that was really encouraging, but nowhere near what our faith had anticipated. Nevertheless, we have many faithful friends who support our ministry of producing cassettes, c.d.'s, songbooks and two autobiographical books. I still do my 'tent-making', i.e.; piano tuning when I'm at home between trips away. Our son Tim is taking more and more of my tunings, and that's as it should be.

When I arrive at my many destinations, people often ask, 'I thought you would bring your dog with you.' I have to explain that I no longer have a guide dog - part of the reason being that a dog needs a reasonably predictable lifestyle. Whether it's a commuter, or a housewife doing her daily shopping, it's territory that the dog has some familiarity with. I go to so many different places; the poor animal would be in a state of continual confusion. Then, too, with the cases of books and cassettes I have to carry, I need both hands, and sometimes wish I had more hands! It's enough to stow my luggage on a crowded train without also having to accommodate a dog.

Years ago, I had occasion to take a large number of records from Cardiff to Belfast by air during the time when I still recorded for Word. I travelled to Ireland for a series of meetings, and needed as many copies as I could carry of my latest recording, Peter Jackson Medleys a compilation of all the recordings I had made for them. The bag checks were very thorough, as always, and when the security officer opened my case to be confronted by a whole array of Peter Jackson countenances staring back at him, he was momentarily startled.

"What's this, boyo?" he said, a trifle caustically, "an ego trip?"

Nowadays, the airport authorities at Cardiff, and, indeed most of the other internal airports, are quite used to seeing me trundling in with my heavy collection of assorted cassettes. In fact, they are very good to me, and I have always been very grateful for the care and attention I receive.

I mentioned this fact once to a very kind air stewardess who was escorting me ahead of all the other passengers to the waiting aircraft.

"You know," I chatted as I held her arm lightly and allowed her to lead me, "I am very impressed with the care you are giving me, and the way that you make sure I'm supervised and looked after. Although, I realise, of course," I joked, "that I am a V.I.P."

"Oh yes?" she said, briefly.

"Yes -" I insisted, " - a Visually Impaired Person!"

"Ah, well," she went on, "we don't think of you so much as that, but more of an M.S.R."

"An M.S.R?" I queried. It was a new one to me.

"A Maximum Security Risk," she said..

"I realise my friends think that," I joked, "but in what way do you think I am a Maximum Security Risk?"

"Well," she went on seriously, "your luggage is standing alone - beside you, but alone. If someone wanted to put something in one of your bags - maybe drugs or a small bomb - you would probably have no idea about it."

It was a sobering thought. Now, whether I am in an airport or a railway station, I always keep my briefcase or bag between my feet where I would feel any movement.

I travel to and from Ireland by air several times each year, but I suppose the most memorable of these flights happened some years ago when I still had Andy, my guide dog. On this particular occasion we were travelling from Southern Ireland in a small twenty-five seat aircraft on a private airline. The weather was every airline passenger's nightmare - very rough with a strong south-westerly wind booming in off the Atlantic. We took off from Cork, and were due to land at Waterford, Dublin and Aldergrove in Belfast.

Soon after we had taken off, the stewardess announced that they would be serving coffee and rolls shortly, but the journey turned out to be so rough that it was impossible to serve anything. The little plane jolted up and down, to and fro in the most alarming manner.

We soon landed at Waterford, and after a brief stop, took off again. The stewardess tried once more. "We shall be serving coffee and rolls shortly," she announced.

We waited, but the constant barrage from the wind told us that we would have to wait a bit longer. The turbulence was the worst I have ever known, and some of the passengers were quite frightened. I did not worry for myself - I determined to enjoy the experience since the cabin staff assured us they had experienced this sort of thing many times before, but I did feel concerned for Andy, lying at my feet. Like a child, he loved the security of a stable world, and stability did not describe our conditions at that moment! I need not have worried, however. He did not seem in the least concerned and remained, soporifically at my feet. In fact, the crew thought he had been heavily sedated.

"Oh, no," I assured them. "I never sedate Andy. That's just him!" They were very impressed. The journey continued, the little aircraft being buffeted and battered by the unrelenting wind. After taking off from Dublin, we heard the usual announcement: "Coffee and rolls will be served shortly." But still they did not appear! In fact, we never did get our promised refreshments. Just before we landed at Aldergrove the stewardess apologised to everyone. "Well, we're very sorry about the coffee," she said, "but you certainly got the rolls!"

She accompanied me to baggage reclaim. I had difficulty dragging my case from the baggage carousel, however, because the handle was broken. I could hardly believe it, but the case had been thrown about with such force, that the thick handle split completely in two!

Perhaps the legendary story concerning the Pope's visit to Southern Ireland came about through similar rough weather. Apparently two labourers were standing nearby as he came off the plane, and one said to the other, "I say, Patrick, did you see what His Holiness did then?"

"Well, what did he do, Seamus?"

"He kissed the ground, so he did."

Seamus looked surprised. "Well, surely, and wouldn't you if you'd just flown Aer Lingus?"

And in case anyone from Aer Lingus happens to read this, I have to add that they have always looked after me very well indeed, and I never have any qualms about flying with them at all!

I should imagine the girl at the check-in desk at New York had a few qualms when the Irishman came up to ask how long it took to fly from New York to Aldergrove.

"Just a minute, sir," she said, turning to look at her timetable.

"Thank you very much!" said Paddy, and walked off.

I'm glad to say, however, that rough flights are comparatively rare, although travelling nowadays does have other irritations in spite of today's technology - or maybe because of it!

Waiting around is perhaps one of the more frustrating effects of travelling today, as I am sure most people would agree. I try to fill up waiting and travelling time by reading or even composing songs. Many a song has been composed on an aircraft as I travel from place to place. (Although they always make me rub it off before I leave..........!)

I have a philosophy about travelling, however. In fact, it does not apply only to travelling, but to being before the public in general. I feel that as a Christian it is very important to keep cheerful, no matter what the provocation. A smile may not always be easy to achieve, but it often creates ease where the situation might otherwise be difficult. In addition, I think that perhaps we ought to declare ourselves as Christians rather more often. It would create something for us to stand by - for it is when others are not aware of what we are, that we are more inclined to let ourselves and our testimony down.

Another time when I was being escorted from the aircraft to the main building at Aldergrove airport, the young lady accompanying me opened a conversation.

"Are you here on pleasure or business, sir?" she inquired pleasantly.

"I'm here on the most pleasurable business in the world," I answered her.

"Oh, what's that?" she inevitably asked.

"I am a diplomat........" I added indirectly, and then, before she could say anything else, I added, "I am an Ambassador for Heaven, because I'm here to communicate the Good News about Jesus."

Having declared my position, a little later, I found myself obliged to stand by it. We arrived at the baggage carousel just as the bags began to appear.

"What colour is your case?" my escort asked. As I have no real conception of colour, this is one of the things I have had to find out, for I realise that colour is very important to sighted people. I told her what my case looked like, but I also mentioned that I have my name printed in Braille under the handle of any cases I carry, so that I can immediately locate them.

On this occasion, we waited and waited, but my case did not seem to be there. I wondered if I had inadvertently given her the wrong description. Finally, only one case circled the carousel. I felt the handle. It was not mine.

Now we had a problem. Had someone taken my case and left theirs? Could I be the innocent victim of an IRA plot? All kinds of fantastic scenarios flashed through my mind. But I had declared myself a Christian. I could not let the side down. I must not panic or lose control. I had to trust God to generate His peace in the situation. A phone call soon solved the problem. A man rang in to say that he had taken the wrong case.

"It looked like mine," he said, "but when I opened it, a pile of Braille books fell out!"

The outcome was that he sent my case on by taxi to the place where I would be staying, and I sent his back. That wasn't quite the end of the incident, because the next time I travelled to Aldergrove a little later that year, the same stewardess met me.

"Oh, I remember you," she said, "you are the ambassador whose luggage got lost."

"That's right, I'm an Ambassador to Heaven," I reminded her.

It pleased me that she had remembered me because of the lost luggage and not because I had got flustered and irritable. If I had protested, she would have remembered me for that; if I had got angry, she would have remembered me for that. But what she remembered was the missing luggage and that I declared myself to be an Ambassador for Heaven. I learned the lesson that we must declare what we are, then stand by it.

CHAPTER NINE

'COME OVER AND HELP US'

MY ASSOCIATION WITH NORTHERN Ireland began back in January 1971. John Blanchard and I went as members of the staff of the Movement for World Evangelisation for a week of coffee bar evangelism. This church-based mission was the vision of the minister the Rev. Derek Poots and Trinity Presbyterian Church, who wanted to try something entirely new. They rented Ballymoney town-hall as a neutral building - a radical idea at the time - and arranged that whilst the coffee-bar was in progress, a prayer meeting would be held in the Orange hall opposite to support the presentation of the Gospel. In those days, the coffee bar culture which had begun in the fifties still existed in Northern Ireland, and we aimed to do what Jesus had done and go to the people who would not come to us.

It was some twenty-six years later that I met Jack, who was introduced to me as the 'right hand man' of the minister of Trinity Presbyterian Church.

"Jack is the elder I trust most of all," said the minister, "and he came to Christ during that coffee bar week in 1971". That introduction to Northern Ireland was the start of twenty-five years (so far) of ministry to the responsive folk in the troubled province of Ulster.

Some people might think that my kind of ministry only happens in churches, but this is far from the truth. As I indicated, Jesus did far more of his preaching to those outside the synagogues than he did in them, and I believe that we should be doing likewise. It was to this end, therefore, that innovation number two came about in that first year in Northern Ireland.

We were invited to minister at a Christian Golfers' Conference in County Donegal. All sorts of highly professional people attended - doctors, professors, and people in high finance, people who owned companies. I was invited to be the main speaker, but I noticed with some trepidation that the very well-known doctor and preacher, Lindsay Glegg, was one of the group of golfers. I was asked to play the piano and minister to these very auspicious people, giving an epilogue every evening after the dinner and presentation of awards for that day.

I remember waking up on the first morning there, with a distinct voice in my head that said, "What are you doing here, Elijah?" I wondered what in the world I was doing in such surroundings! The reply, of course, was "I have been very zealous for the Lord God Almighty......" [5] and I took courage that the Lord had arranged all this, so I would go ahead and enjoy it!

It was not the last Golfers' Conference we were to do. Another took place some time later in Stranraer, Scotland, when we were privileged to stay in the Castle Hotel. These outreaches were a lot of fun, but no one ever took me up on the challenge I threw out to meet me on the golf course to tee off at midnight! I did have a go at playing, actually, but my efforts were woeful. It could be said that I had a handicap - but that was all!

Another lasting memory of the time was the fact that I had apparently put on some weight, for at this time someone informed me, "Let me share this with you, brother: if anyone 'ribs' you about your weight, just tell them that they never put bay windows on slum property!" Like the extra weight, the joke has travelled around with me ever since!

It did not take many visits to Northern Ireland before I came to realise that it had become very special to me. The realisation was put into words one day after my hosts had collected me as usual from Aldergrove Airport. I was due in Enniskillen for a series of meetings, so it surprised me when my driver announced: "Right. First stop - Belfast."

"But I'm supposed to be going to Enniskillen," I protested, puzzled.

"Yes, but you've got a radio interview with Radio Ulster first, and they'd like to do the interview in time for 'Ulster PM'," my host explained. So off we went to the studios. The interview was quite hasty, with a brief talk and a quick play of the piano, but time still remained for one important question.

"We notice that you keep on coming to Northern Ireland," said the interviewer. "Why is that?"

I had to think of a quick answer, and what came into my mind at that moment describes my long association with the province.

"Well, I think it must be that I am in love with Northern Ireland," I told them.

Later, as we drove to Enniskillen, we listened to the programme as it went out. The headline referring to my interview said: 'Gospel pianist in love with Northern Ireland.' In fact, the choice of that head-line also said something about the wonder that is generally felt when folk from mainland Britain choose to visit the province.

It never ceases to amaze me how welcome I am always made to feel, and how grateful everyone is that I have taken the trouble to visit. Their gratitude has always been so humbly effusive that at first, it used to puzzle me. After all, my visits are usually in response to an invitation, and my hosts have always been very generous fi-nancially during my stays in their lovely country, so I feel that it should be me who is the grateful one - as indeed, I am. But still the feeling of wonder permeates from my hosts in grateful thanks.

The answer, I discovered, lies with the troubles that have beset the land. A whole generation has grown up with the constant threat of bombs, discord and danger, and the people became uneasily acclimatised to the fear and uncertainty all around them every day. Over on this side of the Irish Sea we only knew as much as the media presented to us - and that was surely enough - but in Ulster the trouble was unrelenting. One never knew where or whom the next atrocity will strike, so the whole population remained on a constant alert.

Shops had regular bomb drills; store detectives roamed incognito, watching for suspicious characters or abandoned bags; customers' bags were searched on entering.

Certain areas under curfew and patrolling soldiers with guns were common. There have been times when the trouble has been so bad that Belfast was in danger of becoming a ghost city. Meetings became rare, with none at all on Saturdays because of the tension. There were strikes - including electricity - in every area so that one could only cook or use an electric shaver, for instance, during certain times of the day. Those of us on the mainland who are over the age of fifty will find all this reminiscent of the five years of the second World War - years we would dread to live through again. But the folk of Northern Ireland have lived in war-like conditions for more than twenty-five years.

Consequently, they think that no one from the mainland would ever want to visit them. They assume that we will avoid them as much as possible. They cannot understand that anyone would want to travel to Ulster by choice. Amazingly, this does not seem to have fostered a feeling of bitterness or anger towards us, only a wonder and gratefulness when we do visit, that we should bother.

I have shared many a troubled time with my friends in Ulster, and I have been with them when they have suffered some of the worst shootings and bombings. All of which seems to have given an extra dimension to our friendship.

There was one time when the people at my own church pleaded with me not to go to Northern Ireland where I was due in County Armagh for some meetings. There had been a lot of publicity about a shooting, and it looked as though the IRA intended to attack Protestant churches. I listened to what they were saying, but I was adamant.

"I must go," I remonstrated. "Until I get a definite word from them that they do not want me to come, then I will carry on going."

They were very unhappy about my decision, but I could not remain. In the event, the weekend included a houseparty which was attended by twelve ex-terrorists who had become Christians, and it proved to be one of the best times ever.

I particularly love going to Northern Ireland because God is working so greatly there. It is always apparent that where there is persecution, the blessing of God becomes more evident, and some very wonderful things have happened in this troubled province. The Grace of God is particularly evident within the prisons where I have been privileged to speak to the inmates many times.

I usually get into prisons as an entertainer rather than an evangelist. My time with the prisoners usually takes place in the chapel, if they have one, where the piano is most likely to be. The word usually goes round that a blind pianist is to entertain them for an hour. They may not be told that I am a Christian and that my business is to tell them about God's love, but there never seems to be any shortage of people to come in and listen. My method of working is to tell them a little about myself first, and then I play them something. I never begin by declaring my Christianity because it may make them feel trapped and threatened. I simply want first to build a bridge between myself and the men, so that when I come to telling them that they too, are loved by God, they will be open to the suggestion and not shut off by cynicism or anger.

I like to address the men as 'gentlemen'. I feel it is very important to let them know that I am interested in what they are and not what they have done. Then I make them laugh by saying something like: 'I want you to know that I'm just like you. The only difference is that I couldn't see to run so I never tried it on!' They love that! I think that this is one of those times when God uses blindness as a gift - a way in to reach the unreachable.

Once when I went to a young offenders centre in Belfast, I was introduced in the worst possible way. The prison officer said, "Now boys, you've got to be on your best behaviour because this man's blind. If there's any trouble - you'll get it from me, so don't you forget!"

It was terrible! He harangued them, using my blindness as a reason for good behaviour. It put up a solid barrier between us that I would have to begin to break down before they would respond to me at all.

When I stood up to speak, therefore, I said, "Look lads, I know what it's like to be forced to come to chapel. I had to do that for years when I was a kid, so I know exactly what you are feeling." I went on like this, and then I said, "I'm going to play to you and hope that you are really going to respond............" I had to build up their confidence, and the remark about knowing they felt resentful about having to attend chapel did just that. It eased a situation which had become tense and difficult for me. The contrast was so great that I got the attention of every one of the boys. I could feel the warmth from them, confirmed by their handshakes afterwards and sincere expressions of 'Thank you, sir'.

But sometimes, however - especially in The Maze maximum-security prison, the prisoners are not allowed to assemble in any numbers. In this instance, I make use of a piano accordion and go around to play to the men in small groups.

On one of my visits to the notorious Maze prison, as we went in I was asked for means of identification. Security was particularly tight because there had been an incident when someone had got in wearing a priest's robes. As it happened, I hadn't got anything I could offer which would prove my identity.

"Sorry," I joked, "They wouldn't give me a driving licence!"

I thought for a moment that I was not going to be able to go in, but suddenly the friend who accompanied me remembered something.

"Just a minute!" he said, "I've got one of your records in the car - it has your photo on the back. will that do?"

"Yes," said the guard who was something of a wit. "We're very interested in people with records here!"

But when the record had been fetched, we had a further chuckle, because it was entitled, 'Just As I Am', and the guard commented, "Yes, that's just how we take 'em, too!"

On this occasion the chaplain had acquired an undertaking from the men that if I was allowed in, then there would be no trouble, so I went round the compounds with a piano accordion, getting the men singing, and just talking about the Gospel. When I had been all round, they gave me a cup of tea and one of the men came and sat beside me.

"I'm a Christian now," he said, "I wasn't one when I came in here, though. A bomb killed my father and I determined to avenge him, so I was caught carrying a gun. But Jesus Christ found me here, and I am so glad. Now I am praying that others will find him too."

There was a pause, and then he continued, "I am just looking across at a man now. We believe that he will be saved next Tuesday night."

"What?" I said, not quite sure if I had heard aright. "Next Tuesday?"

"Yes," he said, confidently, "that's our Bible Study night when we ask God if he'll be pleased to save a person every Bible Study Tuesday. That man is the next one on the list!"

His confidence in receiving an answer to their prayers led me to think that having someone saved every Tuesday had become a matter or course - and I don't doubt that it really happened, because many men are being saved in the prisons of Northern Ireland. I meet up with them frequently in the prisons, but sometimes after their release, too.

One such case happened not very long ago when I was at the Ulster Temple, a big Elim church in Belfast. A man came to me afterwards and said, "The last time I saw you, I was in the Maze." It really thrills my heart to know that they are going on with the Lord when they have finished their prison sentences.

In another prison in Northern Ireland, the men lined up afterwards to shake hands with me, and I think most of them testified to the fact that they had become Christians since they were inside.

Another time, a prisoner in Winchester prison came to me and said, "I was sitting there listening to you and thinking that it was worth getting into trouble to come in and hear that!"

I used to go to Gloucester prison regularly every six months. One of the prisoners came to me once and said, "Do you know, I've worked it out that I shall see you another three times, with remission!" I feel very humbled when my efforts for the Lord achieve that kind of importance in the lives of needy men.

Often, if I have the men all together, I ask them to choose what they would like to sing. Once, in a Borstal Unit for young offenders, I was asked to play 'Onward Christian Soldiers.' As they were young men, I thought I would take it at something of a 'lick' and spread myself a bit on the piano. I found that the more notes I played, the more heartily they sang, until we got to the chorus of the last verse when they all started to clap and stamp. At that point, half a dozen warders came running in to see what the riot was all about! It was wonderful! We had a great time!

There have been times when I have taken a soloist in with me to entertain - or more accurately, to testify, to the prisoners. However, it is necessary to make sure that they sing the right song......

The legend tells of a singer going in with the accompanist, and he said, "Well, what is your first song?"

"Bless This House," answered the soloist.

"You can't sing that!" said the accompanist, appalled. "What are you going to do when you get to the bit that goes, 'Bless these walls so firm and stout, keeping want and trouble out?' The walls here are meant to keep trouble IN!"

I went to a prison once with the bass soloist, Peter Smith. When I asked him what he wanted to sing, he suggested, 'Let My People Go!' Peter, however, well understands how important it is to choose the right songs, and the prisoners always enjoy his ministry.

One of the greatest surprises I ever had occurred after I had played and talked with the men of The Maze. At the end of our time together, they seemed to collect together and quieten rather formally, and then one of the men stepped forward. He made a moving speech thanking me for my ministry to them and pushed a gift into my hands. I could feel that it was a book. It had no Braille inscription, of course, so I could not read the title, but by its feel, I guessed it to be a Bible printed by 'The Gideons', the organisation who leave Bibles in prisons and other public places.

When I eventually got back to the home of Harold and Meta Patterson with whom I was staying, I showed the gift to them. Opening the cover, they began to laugh.

"What's funny?" I asked.

"Do you know what's written on the flyleaf?" said Meta.

"No, What does it say?"

"It says 'God bless you from the members of the U.D.A. Long Kesh.' The Ulster Defence Association is an illegal organisation, and that's why they are in prison!" (end of insert)

And so God continues to call the most needy from the jails of Belfast. Amid the dreadful difficulty and uncertainty of Ulster, the light shines in the darkest places and men discover the answer to their anger and frustration. It is a sad fact, but I believe it could be argued that there is more actual salvation work going on in prisons than there is in our churches..............

CHAPTER TEN

IT'S FUNNY YOU SHOULD SAY THAT

IT IS AN INTERESTING but unlikely thought that most of the best jokes I ever learned were told me by someone or other in Northern Ireland. One would think, to listen to the news reports in mainland Britain, that Ulster must be a dismal country with little to laugh about. That is far from the truth. True, Ulster has horrendous problems, and the people are deeply concerned and saddened by the situation, but the inherent Irish humour still shines through in spite of the desperation. In fact, it seems to be abundant.

I once did a programme called 'A Taste of Hunni' with Gloria Hunniford on Radio Ulster. She interviewed me between records, and at the same time carried on a 'phone-in' quiz. A lady telephoned in and Gloria asked her the question:

"Can you tell me what 'Aperitif' means?"

The lady on the phone did not quite catch it. "Pardon?" she asked.

"'Aperitif'," repeated Gloria, "What is it?"

"Oh," said the lady, still rather puzzled. "Well, I put mine in a glass overnight."

Now it was Gloria's' turn to be puzzled. "Pardon?" she said.

"A pair o' teef," explained the lady. " I take them out and put them in a glass overnight!"

Another 'radio' story occurred when John Blanchard and I were listening to a friend's radio. We somehow got into a three-way conversation with a man who was talking to the police in Belfast.

"There's mayhem let loose here," he said, excitedly. "Barricades are going up and they're throwing bricks.... and.........oh, there's a guy there now, throwing a petrol bomb. Quickly! You must come quickly!"

"Right. We're on our way," answered the policeman, confidently. A few minutes later, we heard them break into the broadcast again.

"Hello? Hello?" they called, and were reconnected with the caller. "Er....... as a matter of interest, where are you, exactly?"

In the excitement of the moment, the caller had completely forgotten to mention where the trouble was occurring!

On another occasion, we were listening to a news broadcast, and a conversation about incendiary devices. A man was explaining in detail. "You know," he said, "the problem is - it's the explosives that make the bomb so dangerous........!"

One of the first churches I visited in Northern Ireland was Wellington Street Presbyterian in Ballymena. It did not take long to discover that the minister, the Rev. David Alderdyce, while being intensely fervent about the message he preached, was also something of a comedian and would accentuate the points of his sermons with jokes.

"People are too complacent!" he thundered after speaking about the parable of the talents,[6] We should use the gifts the Lord has given us!" Then after a pause, he went on. "Too many people are like the man who went into a pet shop. 'Could I have five hundred fleas and about a hundred cockroaches?' he asked.

'Oh,' said the man behind the counter, 'you'll have to give me a week or so to round them up.'

'That's all right. Indeed, if you have them by the end of the month, I'd be happy enough. I'm moving on the thirty-first, and I have to leave my flat exactly as I found it!'"

"We are content to leave things as we got them," David explained. "There is a lot of cleaning up to do and our ambition is very small. I heard about a man who was so lazy that if he felt cold he wouldn't shiver. But that should not be our attitude. Better the attitude of the man whose aim was that of the old Irish proverb:

"'If I was a cobbler, I'd make it my trade the best of all cobblers to be - If I was a tinker, no tinker beside could mend an old kettle like me.'"

As a true-born Irishman through and through, he told me how he felt about Ireland:

"I'm sure there's nothing strange about a man who sees his own country as unique. Maybe it's the climate, culture or citizens that are dear to us. In my case, I feel Ireland to be that proverbial 'Little bit of Heaven that fell from out the sky..........' While patriotism can be the last refuge of the strong, it is mostly one of the noble things. Few would disagree with the sentiment expressed in the school book of yesteryear: 'I love the bright hills and the green fields of the fair land in which I was born; I love Ireland because it is the place where first I knew a mother's love and a father's care.' Where we come from is very important. It forms part of the moulding of our character."

"Two men were crossing from Ireland to Scotland. They had come from a backward part and had never been at sea before. As they crossed, a storm whipped up and a man fell overboard. The captain announced over the loud speaker, 'Man overboard! Throw out a buoy!' and of course, one of the two men grabbed a young lad and threw him overboard. The captain shouted, 'Don't be stupid! That's not the kind of boy I meant - I meant a cork buoy.' The Irishman replied 'but cap'n, in an emergency like this, does it matter where he's from?'"

"Anything associated with the old country still thrills the Irish emigrant. It was an Irish-American visitor who went to a little village in the south, and there he saw a store where they sold skulls of famous men. He looked round and eyed one he fancied, then asking how much it would be, was told 'one hundred punts'. 'That's a lot for a skull,' he protested."

"'But that's the skull of St. Patrick,' the storekeeper told him, proudly."

"'Oh, well,' said the American, 'I'll buy it because the men in Boston will love it.' So he paid his money, took it, and off he went."

"In about a year's time, he was back in Ireland again, and passing the same little place, he thought maybe he'd go in and see if there was a bargain going. He wasn't so flush with his money this time, but he looked around and spotted a small skull at the end of the shelf."

"'How much for that wee skull there?' he asked the assistant."

"'One hundred punts,' came the answer."

"'That's a lot for a wee skull like that,' complained the American."

"'Oh, aye, but you know,' insisted the man, 'sure and that's the skull of St. Patrick.'"

"'Come off it, ' protested the American, 'you sold me the skull of St. Patrick a year ago.'"

"The shopkeeper smiled. 'Ah, but this is him when he was only a young fella.............'"

It is always good to be encouraged, and in Ireland I have always found great encouragement. "It's like this, Peter," David insisted, "we are deeply in your debt here. Your musical ministry has been such a blessing to us. I only wish you could see your audiences - it would partly repay you to see the enjoyment and blessing on their faces."

I knew a joke was coming on.

"Murphy was tossing and turning, and his wife said, 'Get to your sleep, Murphy.'"

"'I can't,' he replied. 'I've something on my mind.'"

"What's on your mind?" asked his wife.

"'I owe Maguire across the street five hundred pounds and I can't pay it.'"

"'Leave it to me,' said his wife, and opening the window she shouted, 'Maguire! Does my husband owe you five hundred pounds?'"

"'Yes, indeed,' came back the answer."

"'Well, he can't pay it,' shouted back the wife, and she slammed down the window."

"'Now', she said, 'get to your sleep. It's on his mind now!'"

Whatever the joke, the gospel and the need to preach it are never far from David's mind.

"I love stories with a moral," he told me. "That last story says something about having a friend to help, and the benefit of having someone on whom to cast our problem. Our Lord is the greatest friend. '..He took up our infirmities and carried our sorrows......'"

David is the kind of minister who can hold the attention

because no one knows what he will say next. He makes good use of that attention to tell the love of God.

"Of course," he went on, "everyone who has eyes doesn't see the light, and everyone with sight doesn't always use it. A singer was asked, 'Why do you always close your eyes when you're singing?' Shyly she replied, 'I just can't bear to watch people suffering......'"

"This is not the case where you are concerned, Peter. In an age when so much passes for 'music', I can't help thinking about the waiter who dropped a tray of dishes, only to find a few couples on their feet to dance, thinking it was a new release!'"

"No, Peter your music can truly be called music. I know I can express the appreciation of so many here for the work of your hands in writing, your fingers in playing and your lips and your life in testimony. Not everyone is so good at their job."

"A man with one arm went for a shave. The barber, however, was a bit careless and nicked the man's face in several places, having to put plasters on the cuts before offering the mirror. The poor man hardly recognised himself. The barber, only interested in business, simply inquired, 'have you been in here before?'"

'Ah, no,' said his customer, 'I lost that arm in the war!'"

When I finished laughing, David explained.

"You see, Peter, you are accomplished because you had the discipline to practise, which, of course, makes perfect."

"There was a performer in worldly entertainment whose act was to saw women in two. He never made a mistake, and being interviewed, he was asked how he'd become so perfect in his work. 'Well,' he said, 'I practised on the members of my family at home.'"

"'How do you mean?' asked the interviewer."

"'I tried the act out on my brothers and sisters.'"

"'Oh,' said the interviewer, 'how many have you got?'"

"'I have about four half-sisters left......' said the performer.'"

"I have no advice to give you, Peter, on making use of your talents. You might like this story, however......."

"A man came to the owner of a music hall. 'I've got for you an act that will make you popular and prosperous. I've a wee dog that plays the piano.'"

"'I don't believe it,' said the owner."

"'I'll show you,' said the man, and led the dog to the grand piano where it gave a perfect performance.'"

"The owner was about to write a cheque for the act when the visitor said, 'I could make it a double act. I have a wee kitten that sits on top of the piano and sings to the dog's accompaniment.'"

"'Absurd,' scoffed the owner."

"'No, no. Watch this,' and he set the kitten on the piano. The music and singing were a treat."

"'I'll double my offer,' enthused the owner. 'That's a world act. I'll make a fortune with that!'"

"'Aye,' said the man, 'but I don't want you to buy a pig in a poke. Let me tell you the whole truth. That wee kitten doesn't sing a note. The dog is a ventriloquist.'"

I'm afraid I can't go anywhere for long without telling an 'Irish' joke, and some people have asked me how I can tell such jokes when I have such a high respect for the Irish. The truth is that most of the jokes I tell were told to me in the first place by an Irishman - and David Alderdyce knows more than most!

"Paddy the Irishman is known far and wide,' explains David. "He inherits, enjoys and nurtures his precious brand of humour."

"In one school, a teacher was trying to get into her pupils' heads some understanding of pronouns. 'Now,' she said, 'a pronoun stands for somebody. Here's a sentence: 'Mary milked the cow'. What word can you change to a pronoun?'"

"Young Paddy put his hand up. 'The cow, Miss,' he said."

"'How do you make that out?' asked the teacher."

"'Well,' said young Paddy, 'you said that a pronoun stood for somebody. If the cow hadn't stood for somebody, nobody would have any milk.'"

"In another school, the teacher had lost patience and hope with her class. 'You know nothing, yet the minister will be paying a visit next Thursday morning. He'll be asking questions, so don't let me down. He may well ask the simple question, 'Who made you?' Now, does anyone know?' There was no response. 'Well, this is what you are going to do,' said the teacher. 'John, you have a strong voice. If the question comes up, just you stand on your feet and shout out 'God made me!'"

"Sure enough, when his Reverence arrived he said, 'I'm going to start with some simple questions. Who made you?' No one answered. 'Oh, come on,' urged the minister, 'who made you?'. Still no response. He asked again, then after an embarrassing silence, the teacher saw a little red-haired girl raised to her feet."

"Sir,' she said, 'the wee boy that God made isn't here today. He's off with the measles.'"

"Bearing in mind Ireland's association with America, still Paddy does not like 'Uncle Sam' to hurt his pride. An American visited a small farmer who was anxious to show him his stock and crops. First he showed him a dozen big Leicester ewes. The Yank said, 'Those are nice little lambs. If you give them time and good food, in a year or two they should be big sheep like we have at home.'"

"Then the farmer brought him to a field with a lot of big bullocks. He thought he would impress his visitor. But again, the American remarked, 'Lovely little calves,' and advised him that good care and time would make them as big as the animals they had back home. Exasperated, Paddy brought him down the lane towards his humble home, when they witnessed a neighbour's donkey with its head through the fence eating grass. The farmer stepped over and took hold of it, taking its two large ears in one hand and bringing it down with the other. The poor donkey fell at his feet. 'My,' said his companion, who was shocked. 'You were very hard on that poor dumb beast.'"

"'Oh,' said Paddy, 'those wretched rabbits have eaten me out of house and home!' They went on, but before they reached the house, Paddy dug up a few potatoes for dinner."

"The American of course, asked what they were. 'They are potatoes,' the farmer told him." "'Potatoes?' gasped the American, 'back home we grow potatoes ten times bigger than those!'"

"'Ah, maybe,' said Paddy, 'but we just grow them to suit the size of our mouths!'"

"Of course, some people only look on the dark side. For them, every silver lining has a cloud. The doctor told Pat in hospital that he had rabies and that he had only a week to live. 'Get me some paper and a pen,' he requested. The doctor watched him writing frantically. 'Are you writing your will?' he asked.'"

"'Oh no,' said Pat, 'just the names of those I want to bite before I go!'"

"But laughter is good for the soul, and we all enjoy a little entertainment. 'All work and no play makes Jack a dull boy,' and 'the bow that is always bent, ceases to shoot straight.' The Lord loves cheerful people, and tells us that 'a merry heart is as good as medicine'[8] 'A little soda helps the bread to rise, and a little spice adds flavour to the dish.' 'A little icing finishes the cake' - like the man who fell into a tank of varnish. He had a lovely finish."

"Perhaps it's the balance that keeps things right. We don't have to be like the well-balanced Irishman who had a chip on each shoulder. There is a time and a place for everything. 'A word spoken in due season - how good it is! [9] A relevant joke can do more than entertain; it can illustrate like a parable. It can throw light on a window."

"You will remember the vegetarian cat that would only eat cheese - it preferred just to sit at the mouse hole with bated breath. Well, we must use bait to catch both mice and men. A joke at the right moment and in the right place can drive home a point, relieve tension and teach a truth, while out of place it can be a distraction and even an irritation. It can amuse or annoy. There is a time to laugh and a time to cry."

"I have been aware during my ministry of a Scriptural paraphrase which says: 'It is better to eat with those who weep and share the afflicted smart, than to mix with fools in giddy joys that cheat and wound the heart.'"

"Of course, what makes people laugh is revealing. We show more than our teeth when we laugh. We show what turns us on. However, we must take care that our fun hurts nobody. It is necessary to be sensitive and selective when we tell jokes. We must always guard against the unclean."

"'What we say and what we hear needs a sentry at the door of our lips and at the gate of our ear."

David is well into his stride when talking about humour.

"It is also possible to cast our pearls before swine. There are people to whom the joke must be explained, and this spoils it all. It becomes like the man reading the dictionary. He said it was an interesting book, but a bit cumbersome as it stopped to explain every word."

"Paddy the Irishman appears smart at times and gives the answer that brings him out on top."

"An Englishman, Irishman and Scotsman were in a desert place together and bored stiff with their surroundings. Then one happened to find an old rusty tin box. He kicked it, and inadvertently released a genie that was so glad to be released that he promised the fulfilment of a wish to each of the three. The Englishman quickly said, 'I wish I was home,' and instantly he found himself back in England's green and pleasant land. The Scotsman followed with the request that he, too, would love to see his ain folk, and in a flash he was back in bonnie Scotland. As Paddy stood with his finger in his mouth, the genie said, 'Have you no wish?'"

"'Oh yes,' said Paddy, 'I was just thinking: I'm going to be very lonely here. Could I have them two fellas back?'"

David pulls no punches when talking about the Irish.

"Sometimes Irish men can be awkward: Like two bald men fighting over a comb."

"Then again, Irishmen have been accused of being easy-going. A planeload of men who had been unemployed for years, touched down to build a wall in the desert. Paddy became worried when he saw the mountains of sand all around. He said to his mates, 'come on - let's get home quickly before they bring the cement and water.'"

"There had been a hammer throwing competition. The Englishman came second, but the Irishman came first, beating all records. Indeed, they couldn't even find the hammer! Both men were interviewed, and asked how they managed to do so well. The Englishman said, 'Well, my father worked in the mines and developed strong muscles shovelling coal. I've worked hard all my days, too, shovelling coal. That's why I was successful in coming second.' Then when they asked Paddy how he came first, he said, 'I never worked a day in my life, and my father before me never worked either. Indeed, I'm told that my grandfather used to say that if anybody ever put a hammer in your hand, throw it as far away as you can, and I've been following his advice all my life.'"

"Pat hadn't been too well, and they thought he might get a light job in England. He was eventually sent to a building site where he began work as a labourer. The foreman handed him a pick and shovel and asked him to dig a hole twelve feet wide and twelve feet deep. 'Ah,' said he, 'I couldn't do it, I'm not fit.'"

"'Don't worry,' said the foreman,' we'll get you a JCB.'"

"'Ah, now,' said Pat, 'what good's a medal when you're dead?'"

"Talking about holes, there was a team of Irishmen who were working below the surface in the centre of London. Someone heard the singing and the general jocularity. On getting their attention, he inquired, 'What's going on down there?'"

"An Irish voice yelled back, 'We're celebrating!'"

"'O, asked the man, 'is it the foreman's birthday or something?'"

"'No, shouted the worker, 'it's the third anniversary of the hole!'"

"There are others who are prepared to tackle anything in the right spirit, like the Irish plumber who, when he was on holiday, visited the Niagara Falls. He stepped back and considered what was before him. 'You know,' he said, thoughtfully, 'I think I could fix that.'"

"I'm sure it is better to be an optimist than a pessimist. The best example I know of super-optimism is when a lady in the church pew slips on her shoes again when she hears the minister say "Finally, brethren...."'"

"Whatever reputation the Irishman seems to have acquired, he is, as a general rule, very generous. There are always exceptions, however. In the County of Antrim is a small town where a pair of rare birds was seen. The council decided to find out where these birds nested and bred. So they offered a reward. Two Ballymena men keen for the reward packed their bags to follow the birds. They pursued them right to the North Pole, and realising that they would have to wait a while for the breeding season, they pitched their tent. In the meantime, as the weeks passed the folk at home were worried that there had been no word from the men. However, the only volunteers who offered to track them down were members of the Red Cross. In due course, they found them at the Pole, and seeing the pinnacle of the little tent, they shouted, 'Anybody there?'"

"A Ballymena voice called back, 'Who is it?'"

"'The Red Cross,' came the reply."

"'Go away,' shouted one of the men. 'We gave to you last year!'"

"Some folk here may not be any more generous in their affection for the English. Seamus was in for the 'Brain of Britain' contest, and the questions were put to him."

"'First question, Seamus. What was the date of the Battle of the Boyne?'"

"He thought for a moment and then said, 'Pass.'"

"'Second question, Seamus. Who fought at the Battle of the Boyne?'"

"'Pass', came the quick reply."

"'Third question. Who won the Battle of the Boyne?'"

"'Pass,' said Seamus yet again."

"At this a little man in the audience shouted with great gusto, 'Good man, Seamus. Tell 'em nothing!'"

"Irishmen do have their way of expressing things. A young Irishman proposed to his intended. 'How would you like to be buried with our family?' he asked. Then they were out for a walk one evening and the church bells rang. 'Why did the bell ring tonight, John?' asked the young lady.'"

"'Because I love you,' replied John, romantically.'"

"Another night they were walking along the same road and the bell rang. 'Why is the bell ringing tonight?' she asked again."

"'Because I'm going to marry you,' he said."

"In the course of time they did marry, but a few years later they were walking along the same road again. This time the church bell rang and the wife said, 'Why is the church bell ringing, John?'"

"'Because there's someone pulling the rope!'" replied the husband."

"What a pity things change so much. We do well to examine ourselves and remember that 'a garden without attention will grow weeds' and 'if we want to get honey, we should not kick the hive or forget the flowers.' If you've got a helpmate, tell her. Show her your love. Her price is above rubies. In these days too many have roving eyes. A man was singing at a function and he noticed a lady watching him intently. Afterwards he said to her, 'I noticed you were watching me. Should I know you, or do you know me?'"

"'Oh, no,' she said, 'but you are very, very like my third husband.'"

"'Really,' he said. 'Have you been married three times?'"

"'No,' she answered, cannily, 'just twice.'"

"Our world would remain a happier place if people would remain faithful until death do us part. She may not be an oil painting, but she may have a heart of gold. There's another story about a genie who was set free by a farmer who found an old bottle in his barn. 'How can I reward you?' he asked the farmer.'"

"'Well, I have a wee dog,' said the farmer,' and I'm entering him for a show next week. Could you ensure that he wins?'"

"The genie went to the kennel to look at the dog and was horrified to see that he had only three legs, one eye, no tail, and was mangy and sickly. He returned to the farmer and said, 'Could you not find something a bit easier for me? I'm a bit rusty as yet.'"

"The farmer said, 'Well, my wife is entering a beauty contest tomorrow and she's indoors trying to make the best of her appearance. Could you help her to succeed?'"

"The genie took a look at the farmer's wife and rushed back to the farmer. 'Ah, sir,' he panted, 'Can I have another look at the wee dog?'"

"Talking about dogs, a man had his dog so well trained that when it walked backwards it would wag its tongue at people. Not like the lady's dog that was so spoilt that when they travelled in the train, it would occupy a seat next to its proud owner. An American tourist wished to take the seat from the dog, but the look from the lady sent him further along the train to look for another seat. After an unsuccessful search he returned, caught the dog by the tail and threw it out of the window. He was almost devoured by the distraught lady. A gentleman opposite lifted up his eyes, put down his book and said to the tourist, 'You Americans are amazing people. You drive on the wrong side of the road; you eat your food with a fork in the wrong hand, and now you've thrown the wrong female out of the window.'"

Neither do ministers miss the lash of David Alderdyce's jokes. I always remember this one when I am preaching:

"The preacher was still going strong when a man headed for the door."

"'Where are you going?' called the minister from the pulpit."

"'I'm going for a hair cut,' called back the man."

"'Could you not have had that before you came in?' asked the preacher.'"

"'I didn't need it then,' came the prompt reply."

"Then there was the minister who called one day just as a row raged between the lady of the house and a painter who had watered down the emulsion. The lady thought her minister was heaven sent when he said, 'Leave this to me.' His advice to the painter was not quite quoted from the Bible: 'Re-paint and sin no more.'"

It is not David's usual way to pervert the Scripture, but it certainly makes one think again of the truth of the Bible! But he had not yet finished with clergymen.

"As a Presbyterian, there can be no harm in relating the story of the bishop who was as unpopular as a pork sausage in a synagogue. One day a curate called. The Bishop's maid answered the door. 'Could I see the Bishop?' asked the curate."

"'Did you not hear?' replied the girl, 'The Bishop's dead.'"

"'Oh,' said the young man and went away. He returned in an hour or so. 'Any chance of a word with the Bishop?' he asked again."

"The maid was puzzled. 'Did I not tell you he was dead?' she said."

"'Oh yes, of course,' said the young man and went away. He returned again in an hour's time. 'I just wanted a wee word with the Bishop,' he repeated."

"Now the girl was annoyed. 'Haven't I told you a number of times? He's dead,' she said in exasperation."

"'Surely, but I couldn't hear it too often,' grinned the curate, happily."

"This reminds me of Pat and William who had worked together for years. William couldn't tell the time, but Pat did his best to explain the hands' movements."

"After a period of instruction, William seemed happy, and was expressing his gratitude when Pat said, 'Just before you go, there's another wee thing maybe you should know. Some clocks have Roman numerals.'"

"'Ah, Pat,' says he, 'sure and are you going to bring religion into it now after us being very good friends for years?'"

Services in Wellington Street Presbyterian Church are not dull affairs! Part of my ministry is to encourage ministers who have a consecutive ministry. I've met any amount of these men and women of God who have a week by week ministry in the church. Of course, there are many stories.

A minister who got up in the pulpit showed signs of having had a fight with his razor that morning. He was covered in bits of plaster and cotton wool. He felt he ought to apologise.

"I'm so sorry," he said, "but while I was thinking about my sermon, I cut my face rather badly."

"One of his congregation said to him afterwards, 'Perhaps in future, Pastor, you should think more about your face, and cut your sermons!'"

There was also a story about a farmer who sat through a harvest festival. He heard the vicar say, 'There's a sermon in every blade of grass.'"

Next day the farmer saw the vicar mowing his lawn. 'That's right, vicar, " he said, "keep 'em short!'

Another man looked for the vicarage in a village. He asked a local where it could be found. The reply was, "Oh, you don't mean the vicarage, you mean the rectory."

Having received the instructions, he went on, but he had to ask again. The next person said, "You don't mean the rectory, you mean the vicarage." By the time he found the house and pressed the bell, the man was thoroughly confused. When the minister came to the door, he was greeted with, "Excuse me, is this the victory or the wreckage?"

When I visited the Mountains of Mourne in Northern Ireland, I heard this gem: A minister had been in his church in a farming area for about thirty years. The farmers were so tired with all their outdoor work that the minister knew very well that most of them had a snooze during his message. Eventually he retired and a younger man took his place. They met one day and the retired minister asked how he was getting on.

"Oh, very well," said the new man.

"How do you manage with the farmers? Can you keep them awake?"

"Oh, yes, I keep them awake all right."

"How do you do that?"

"Well, in the opening prayer I ask that God will grant us to know his presence, then in the intercession time I ask that God would grant his blessing on the royal family and ministers of the crown. Then just before I preach I ask that God will grant his blessing upon what I'm going to say, and then in the benediction I ask him to grant his blessing on our homes. You see, with all that talk of grants, the farmers keep awake all right!"

An unmarried young curate was strikingly handsome, and therefore a very eligible bachelor. When he got up in the pulpit to preach, all the equally eligible girls used to smile at him and even wink, making it quite obvious they were interested in him.

The young man was embarrassed and said to his vicar, "Look, I think I should move on, because this is a real problem." He did go, and another young curate took his place. He was not at all good looking, and got on fine.

At a retreat one day, the two curates met up. The first one asked how the other was managing. "Fine," he said.

"What about the girls - do you have any problems with them?"

"Oh, no," said the young man, "I believe in safety in numbers, you see."

"Oh," said his friend, "I believe in safety in Exodus.......!"

Then there was Seamus who came back from a pilgrimage to Lourdes. When he arrived at customs, the officer said to him, "What have you got in that bottle?"

"Oh, that's the holy water - the holy water from Lourdes."

"I'll take a look at it," said the customs official.

He screwed off the top, sniffed and said, "That's whiskey!"

Seamus threw his hands into the air excitedly. "Another miracle! Another miracle!"

And finally brethren..........

A lady had her handbag snatched, but she had a good look at the thief. So the policeman said, 'Would you know him if you saw him again?'

'I would, surely,' assured the lady.

An identification parade was therefore arranged, and all the men were lined up. As the lady walked along the line, Paddy jumped out and said, 'That's her!'

CHAPTER ELEVEN
CHALLENGING BLINDNESS

CHALLENGING BLINDNESS IS THE motto used by the Royal National Institute for the Blind to describe their attitude towards blindness. Through all its many far-ranging services in education, employment, social welfare, lobbying for the rights of blind people, and the provision of specially adapted domestic aids, it regards blindness as something to overcome, and we, in this country, are fortunate indeed to have such a charitable organisation to champion our cause and facilitate our difficulties.

In the context of this book, it would be quite impossible to do justice to the work of 'The NIB' as we call it. All I can hope to do in these few pages is to show you what 'The NIB' means to me.

The acronym 'NIB' is not quite accurate, for it received royal patronage in 1875, then a Royal Charter in 1948. The 'Royal' part of the name was included finally in 1953. Even so, familiar usage dies hard, and most blind people will know what you mean when you ask them about 'The NIB'.

Long before I was aware of its existence it had strong relevance and a major influence in my life. The 'Sunshine Homes' I attended at Leamington Spa and East Grinstead were constituted and run by the then National Institute for the Blind. As to how I managed to attend both 'Homes' as a baby? Well, that's a story I just can't resist telling.......

Leamington Spa's Sunshine House, as my parents knew it, was situated some twenty or so miles from where we lived in Birmingham. It seemed obvious, therefore, that I should reside there as a two-year-old. However, whilst there, a decision was made in the higher echelons of the NIB that all the precocious, bright, intelligent and promising children should be transferred to East Grinstead in Sussex. All the not-so-bright babies should remain at Leamington spa together with children who unfortunately had some extra handicap. Thus I found myself at East Grinstead!

In fact, though, when I heard about this in later years, I was quite surprised. I have always considered myself to be a slow developer, not always adept at grasping a situation, or being able to weigh things up straight away. Neither do I recall having a particularly high Intelligence Quotient when we did the tests as children.

It's perhaps worth pointing out here that the educational needs of blind children have undergone many changes. The medical condition, measles, which caused my blindness has now been largely overcome in the West, as too, has a surfeit of oxygen to premature babies that used to cause partial loss of sight. Conversely, though, those blind and extra handicapped babies who didn't survive previously now do survive due to the progress of medical science. This means that the education of these handicapped children is quite a different matter from the education I received as a child. There is also the somewhat controversial tendency to integrate handicapped children into mainstream schools rather than to give the specialised education which we 'enjoyed'.

When I graduated from the Sunshine Home at East Grinstead to the Birmingham Royal Institution for the Blind just eight days before my fifth birthday, I soon started to learn Braille - all the materials being supplied by the NIB. Every aspect of education was covered: special apparatus for arithmetic; relief maps for geography; Braille books and even specially adapted toys. Always, when we opened a study book, or a Braille music book with which to learn our examination grade pieces, or when simply reading for pleasure, we would find on the first page: Printed and published by the National Institute for the Blind, 224 Great Portland Street, London, W1.

And now, as an adult, although there are other sources for books such as the Scottish Braille Press in Edinburgh; the National Library for the Blind in Stockport; The Torch Trust for the Blind in Market Harborough - which has the most comprehensive collection of Christian books in this country - I still depend for most of my needs on the NIB. As the needs of the visually handicapped have been developed and assessed, so has the NIB bravely attempted to keep up in terms of the accessibility of its many services.

In more recent years, the Institute has moved its main premises to Peterborough whilst still retaining offices and a resource centre in London. There is a 24-hour answering service, so that orders can be placed which are attended to by 'Customer Services' each weekday morning.

The NIB has an intensive magazine programme, ranging from Television and Radio Times plus Classic FM, and magazines to do with shopping, physical fitness, blind welfare, and occupations such as piano-tuning and physiotherapy; information technology, and lists of latest published books and cassettes, to name but a few. These publications keep us updated on all the new developments in technical aids. I use some of these.

For instance, sometimes I will make myself coffee, or prepare my own breakfast cereal. In order for me to tell just how much water is going into the cup or mug, I use a 'Liquid Level Indicator'. This device has a short probe between two longer ones. When placed over the edge of the cup so that the probes are actually in the cup at a certain level, as soon as the liquid comes into contact with the two longer probes, an intermittent bleep is emitted together with a vibration pulse. (The latter is particularly helpful to deaf-blind people.) Then, when the liquid hits the centre, shorter probe, one hears a continuous sound plus a continuous vibration. This provides me with a way of knowing when the container is half full or nearly full.

As I travel around, I often have to stay in people's homes. Sighted people will, of course, invariably turn on the light when they show me to my room. Then, when they leave me to cope, they don't like to think that they are 'leaving me in the dark'! (Of course, it's not 'dark' or 'light' to me - it's just normal!) After my host has gone, I would normally have no idea whether the light has been left on or not - and two-way switches can be very deceiving!

In order to obviate this problem, a device known as a 'Light Probe' has been developed. It's a small object with a light sensor which, when switched on, emits a sound, and the stronger the light source, the higher the pitch of the sound, and vice versa. Before I acquired this technical wonder, I had, I'm sure, on a number of occasions slept the night through with a light on!

It was winter. The darkness had already shrouded the little village where I had to take the weekend services. The young minister escorted me upstairs to my room. I noticed him groping with much difficulty for the light switch. "Excuse me," I said, "I'll help you," and I switched on the light with no trouble! We both laughed till our sides ached, and I'm sure he has related that story over and over again.

In our kitchen we have a talking microwave oven. It tells me about cooking modes, times and even when the door is open or closed. In our bathroom we have talking scales which tell Margaret and me how we're faring in the 'Battle of the Bulge'! So many wonderful things - not necessarily to make life easier, but rather to enable people like me to be more efficient in spite of our disability.

There are people who are far more into information technology than I am, yet none of us would be able to use a computer without a speech screen-reader. Whatever we put on the screen is read back to us - a great deal different from my typing days when I could never be the adjudicator of what I had written. Fortunately for me, a very close friend, John Barker, is training me. John was the computer training officer for East Dyfed Health authority.

One day in 1991 I was reading a magazine published by the R.N.I.B., when I came across an advert announcing an information technology exhibition in Bristol. It concerned computers, Braille embossers, and many other things about which I hadn't the remotest clue. I asked John, "Do you fancy coming with me to Bristol to see what this is all about?" He jumped at the idea, and we set off for Bristol little knowing of the impact that was about to be made on our lives.

We arrived at the exhibition in good heart - John is a tonic to be with - and we have so much in common: our love of words, our addiction to radio in its heyday, and not least, the fact that we attend the same church. We are friends in the truest and fullest sense of that word.

It was a day of mind-boggling discovery. I had literally no idea of the developments and progress of technology for the visually impaired. But John's computer mindset quickly sized up the situation, assessed the enormous potential for me, and said, "You've gotta go for this, Jacko!"

All the way back to West Wales we talked of nothing else, and I spent a relatively sleepless night, having been over-stimulated by the excitement of seemingly endless possibilities which were about to open up for me. But in my mind was the big question: how could I possibly afford such expensive technology which would include a printer, a Braille embosser, a monitor and a computer - not to mention the specialist software?

Again the NIB came to my rescue, this time in the form of their employment officer who came to my home to assess my problems and needs. I showed him all the bulky Braille folders of stored piano-tuning customer data - my wardrobe was gradually being taken over! He was impressed and suitably horrified. "You could have all this information stored on disk, and retrieved when needed at the touch of a button," he informed me. The prospect was dazzling, and so, thanks to this very helpful representative from the NIB, I waited with bated breath for the culmination of the process which would bring ignorant me into the age of information technology.

Some time later, therefore, via the local employment services a quantity of hardware arrived at my house. It was to be loaned to me until such time as I could replace it with upgrades of my own. Then, since they had generously loaned me their equipment, they were rather obliged to show me how to use it! So basic training from the Employment Services followed, but the only thing going for me was the fact that I could type - something I had learned to do way back in college days - otherwise I was absolutely clueless. I made virtually no progress until John came to my rescue.

One of the great things about John is that he has the knack of getting into a blind person's shoes and seeing things from our point of view. Add to this the fact that we enjoy each other's company immensely, and I began to progress slowly.

John would teach me some application and then leave me for two or three weeks so that I could use it until I knew it, little by little, precept upon precept - and if I got stuck, I needed only to lift the receiver and my problem was solved!

At about this time, John was made redundant due to the inevitable cutbacks in the Health Service. It was a big blow for him, for he was at an age when nobody wanted him in spite of his experience and savoir faire. For me, of course, it meant that he could give me more intensive training.

John always reckoned that while he was teaching me, he was all the time learning himself. He took a course with the R.N.I.B. in learning Braille - no easy accomplishment for a person in their early fifties. Then eventually he set up his own company - and because of all his experience gained in training me, he now trains visually handicapped people all over England, Wales and Scotland. He says that he's busier than he's ever been in his life, and tells me, "it's all your fault!"

Every year John and I go to Birmingham for the day to attend an exhibition of technology for the visually impaired. It is one of the biggest exhibitions of its kind, and it provides us with an opportunity to keep abreast of the technological revolution.

Sometimes life throws up some whimsical surprises. This annual exhibition is held in Queen Alexandra College, Harborne - the very place where I started in Kindergarten, aged almost five years!

The first time we made this annual pilgrimage to Birmingham, I stood in a room that had once been very familiar to me. A young lady inquired interestedly, "Are you a Braille user?"

I replied, "Over half a century ago I started learning Braille in this very room!"

The NIB will always have its critics, but whenever I hear of such criticism, or maybe when I am tempted so to criticise, I ask the question that I wish others would ask: "Where would we be and how would we cope without such a body - always Challenging Blindness"?

CHAPTER TWELVE
A VITAL SERVICE

BACKING UP AND COMPLEMENTING the work of the RNIB is the National Library for the Blind. Having been introduced to it during my youth, I have been taking advantage of the service ever since. And so it is that at frequent intervals, the postman's bundle of letters is considerably enlarged by a bulky, distinctive bag which, with its Braille inscription indicates that it contains written matter for the blind, and therefore will travel through the post free of charge. Inside the bag will be one or two volumes of a book that I have ordered from a long list.

Every day, a Royal Mail van drives up to the loading bay of the Royal National Library for the Blind at Bredbury, Stockport, to collect several hundred of these special bags. Each one will be delivered to subscribers, while every day hundreds are received back in return, to be re-filled with the next book choice.

The Library for the Blind began its vital service only about thirty or so years after Louis Braille devised the system of raised dots that would enable the blind to read. In 1882, therefore, a maiden lady, Miss Martha Arnold, who was herself blind, elicited the help of her friend, Carlota Howden, later Mrs. Dow, and the two ladies set up a library service of Braille books in a room of Miss Arnold's house in Hampstead.

At the time, the blind had very little access to literature. The Braille method of reading having so comparatively recently been invented, nearly all reading matter had to be transcribed by hand and the process took a great deal of time and effort.

This solution concerned Miss Arnold who aimed that a library would 'bring solace and light' to the blind, and that it should help to 'raise their literary standard'. So the two ladies gathered together a collection of fifty books, and with ten subscribers the service began. They set a general annual charge of four shillings and fourpence, with a larger charge for those who could afford it; but it was still a huge amount at a time when the average annual wage for a servant would be only sixteen pounds a year. Blind people could rarely find paid work, anyway.

Some help came in the form of Messrs. Carter Paterson, who arranged to carry books for fourpence in the Greater London area, but even this presented an insuperable problem to an impoverished blind person of the 1880's who might need two deliveries of books each month. It was necessary, therefore, for Miss Arnold to solicit voluntary contributions in order to keep the service going. This she did, and although finances were always tight, the library of books kept growing, and the number of blind subscribers continued to increase. By 1895 the library served 300 readers with a stock of 3,200 volumes, and Miss Arnold had to move house twice!

When the indomitable lady died in 1898, she left a well-established service, which could now benefit from an Executive Committee with the illustrious help of the Rt. Hon. James Bryce as President, and Lady Frederick Cavendish as Vice-President.

The new committee found itself beset by many problems as it struggled to stabilise the service, but even so, by 1904 the stock of books had grown to nearly 8,000 volumes, with a yearly addition of more than 500. But with the expansion, running costs rose to over £800 per year and adequate premises had to be found in an adapted shop and basement in Bayswater.

In 1906, the committee appointed Miss Ethel Austin, another maiden lady, to the post of Secretary and Librarian, and a new era in the life of the Library for the Blind began. Against very considerable odds, including the persistent financial burden and the upheaval of the First World War, Miss Austin managed to keep the service going.

In 1908, special postage rates were granted for the blind, and gradually the Library spread to engulf the entire Bayswater Road premises.

By 1915, approaches were made to the Carnegie United Kingdom Trust - which had already paid for and presented 4,000 volumes of books produced by the National Institute for the Blind - to ask if they would help to finance new and even better premises. So, in 1916, the Library moved into specially adapted premises in Tufton Street, Westminster, of which £10,000 of the cost was paid by the Trust, and a further £6,000 from special appeals. In the same year, the service became free for all blind readers; its name changed to 'The National Library for the Blind'; it obtained exemption from rates, and Lord Shaw of Dunfermline, chairman of the Carnegie United Kingdom Trust, became Chairman of the Executive Committee.

Another year saw the Library of Manchester and Salford Blind Aid Society joined with the National Library, and soon more new premises meant a branch became established in the north. Miss Austin died suddenly in 1918, and by this time the annual expenditure had risen to £6,000 with the annual circulation of volumes standing at nearly 100,000.

By 1928 the Library, with a great deal of help from the Carnegie Trust and other voluntary contributions, had enlarged premises in Great Smith Street, London; extended premises in Westminster, and had also suffered in the disastrous Thames Floods in January of that year. Finances continued to be critical until Local Authority grants began to improve the situation, eventually forming more than 40 per cent of the entire financial burden, including help with payments to proof-readers and copyists.

And so the Library thrived - not without many problems, most of which were, and still are, financial - but it has nevertheless continued to expand over the years. A landmark occurred in 1952 when Her Majesty the Queen became patron, and in June 1957, Her Majesty Queen Elizabeth the Queen Mother visited the annual Reading competition.

The financial situation came to a head in 1975 when the accounts showed a deficit of £40,000 which equalled a third of the annual income. Urgent action had to be taken, and it was eventually decided that costs would be improved if the whole service could be housed under one roof.

After a thorough search, the warehouse in Bredbury, Stockport, became available, and in 1978 the whole Library changed location again to be housed in these excellent premises.

Finances continue to be provided mainly from voluntary sources and so are always a problem,[10] but the present stock now consists of 40,000 books. The actual number of volumes, however, amounts to a good deal more when it is borne in mind that one book printed in Braille will necessarily consist, on average, of several volumes, and maybe up to ten or so. (The Oxford Children's Encyclopaedia takes up 59 volumes!)

And so blind readers continue to enjoy access to more and more books.

The service, however, cannot continue without the help of voluntary, dedicated proof-readers, most of whom are sighted and have learned Braille for the purposes of this work. I know the importance of this task since I experienced some proof reading on behalf of 'The Torch Trust for the Blind'. But when Margaret saw a programme on television called 'The Human Factor' and recorded it for me to listen to, it set off a chain of events which resulted in me undertaking to proof read for a very special Braille translator.

The programme told the story of a convicted murderer who started life with the name, John Cheeseman. An insecure childhood produced behavioural problems that led him into approved schools, borstals and prisons for most of his life. He described himself as 'rather a wild lad', who made his first appearance in court at the age of eight for stealing a bicycle, moving steadily on through various hostels and approved schools until the age of fourteen. At this time an incident occurred which was to focus his anger and feelings of insecurity.

While his mother was in hospital, John stayed with his married elder brother, Joe, whom he adored. During this stay they visited friends of his brother's, and with a terrible shock of realisation, John heard himself described as Joe's 'adopted brother'. He had no idea up to this point that his 'Mum' was not his natural mother, and the news shook him to his very soul. He felt let down, rejected and particularly betrayed by Joe, whom, he thought, could never have accepted him as a brother from the start.

In an instant, all the love he had for his family turned to hatred and mistrust, and if he had any respect at all for authority before, it disappeared completely now. He became totally lawless and vicious so that within a short time he found himself inevitably in prison.

By the age of fifteen he had become so dangerous that he was confined in Rampton Special Hospital. Three years later he attacked a male staff nurse with an iron bar, and consequently received a twenty-year Restriction Order. The next five years were spent mainly in seclusion while being drugged with tranquillisers, but nothing made any difference to the deep-seated feelings of hate and anger that could only find their expression in violence.

At one point he had a last chance to break the round of sedation and seclusion. He was taken off all the drugs and given a responsible job in the ward kitchen and stores. Then someone considered that Broadmoor Special Hospital might help him, and he was transferred there, but he did not cope very well, and soon found himself returned to Rampton where he was put to work in the bakers.

Suddenly he seemed to be making good progress. He worked well and graduated to decorating special occasion cakes. Then, just as the future looked brighter, another crisis occurred.

He had improved so much that it was thought appropriate to consider his release. However, just at that time, public opinion ran very high over another prisoner who faced possible release. The Review Board could not risk an outcry, and John's release was refused. Now he abandoned himself to violence. He had no interest in the consequences - he felt only hate for all around him.

In 1974, when he was in his thirties, he attempted to kill an inmate with a knife that resulted in the sentence 'to be detained without limit of time'. Three years later the murder that had hovered dangerously near for so long finally happened, and he received a life sentence for his part in the death of another patient.

Now he tried to use the system to suit himself. He took drugs, held hostages and did all he could to wreak revenge on everyone. In addition, he secretly stored a list of all the injustices he felt he had received by adding them, one by one, to a 'Box of Hatred', which he decided to use against the prison system if ever he should be released. His long collected records were so extensive that he considered that it could be the most comprehensive documentation on the penal system and its rules ever collected by a prisoner. He became adept at 'playing the system'. In fact, at one point he even instituted legal proceedings against the Home Secretary and this resulted in one of the statutory prison rules being changed!

His 'Box of Hatred' became so important to him that he never allowed it out of his possession. It was his sole purpose for living.

Then in 1983 he appeared in a television documentary called Lifer. As a result he received letters from various people, one of whom was a lady called Margaret who claimed to be a Christian and told him she and a friend were praying for him. It did not impress him at all.

Some time later he noticed an almost imperceptible difference in his own attitude. His behaviour had not substantially changed - he still got into trouble, but he began to see something that he had not noticed before in the general demeanour of one of the prisoners. From time to time, the two men chatted, and John discovered that Peter had become a Christian. 'Jesus has his hand on my life,' he told John, 'and I am convinced that you, too, will become a Christian one day.' John scoffed at the idea, and declared he was an atheist and would not become a Christian in a thousand years. He remembered the conversation very vividly just a short time later when he knelt in his cell and begged the Lord Jesus Christ to come into his life and change him. The power of God had broken through all the determination and hatred, and had begun the changing process that he so desperately needed. Then, in order to put the past behind and look towards a new future, he decide a he needed a completely new name, and so chose David Lant.

From that moment on, with what seemed to be a new identity combined with his new name, his attitude improved in leaps and bound. Then one night he awoke in the early hours and found himself whistling a tune. When, at dinnertime the next day he was still whistling it, his friend, Peter, tackled him about it.

"Do you know what that tune is?" he asked. David had no idea. Peter fetched his hymnbook and opened it. "There," Peter showed him, "To God be the Glory." David looked at the words of one verse in particular:

O perfect Redemption, the purchase of blood,
To every believer - the promise of God.
The vilest offender who truly believes,
That moment from Jesus a pardon receives.

It fitted his situation exactly. People had been praying for him, and God had been working. The old John Cheeseman had become the new David Lant and had receive forgiveness for his many sins; and the Holy Spirit had come into his life to start the changing process.

Now everyone around him could see that something had happened to this desperate character. To begin with he smiled and laughed! There had not been much laughter in his life up to that point. But now his attention was focused on God and the burden of hate lifted from his shoulders. He was free to love and be loved. Now, instead of seeking revenge on all around him, he sought ways in which he could help his fellow men.

By now he had been moved to Parkhurst Prison, and the assistant chaplain there had a suggestion which he wondered if David would like to take up. The Royal National Institute for the Blind needed people who could transcribe books into Braille for their readers. It would entail learning Braille, of course, and acquiring a machine to print out the Braille characters.

Amazingly, the money for the machine was provided, and David set to learning Braille. He found it hard work but be succeeded, and now transcribes books on a more or less full time basis, although he changed from the RNIB to transcribing for The Torch Trust for the Blind who could offer him better opportunities for his work.

I listened to the documentary with wonder. It was another of those remarkable stories that we hear about form time to time. But this had a connection to me in a small way. I might perhaps be reading some of the books that David Lant had transcribed into Braille. I felt I would like to meet him, but as Parkhurst is a maximum-security prison, I would need permission. I wrote to the chaplain, giving him details about myself, and received the requested permission to visit.

Some time later, during a visit to Eastney Evangelical Church, near Portsmouth, I travelled over to the Isle of Wight to see David Lant.

We had a good time together and I came away promising to help him with his Braille transcriptions. He needed proof readers who could spot any mistakes before the books went into print, and someone like myself who had grown up reading only Braille, could be of valuable help to him. Although I have very little time to spare as I combine my work as a piano tuner with my ministry around the country, I do try to help David as much as possible by proof reading as I travel to and from my various destinations.

It has been good to see that time is proving the fact of David's transformation from a bitter and hardened criminal to a useful and fulfilled citizen, as he continues his work from prison. It may be also, that with the continued and obviously established change in his life, the Review Board might consider his release in the future. After a lifetime in an institution, it may be that David will require our prayers even more then.

CHAPTER THIRTEEN
THE MINISTRY OF MUSIC

A LARGE PART OF MY ministry takes the form of accompanying singing. Wherever I go to minister, before I do any speaking, I am usually asked to accompany the congregational singing. That is - I am *now*. There was a time, many years ago when I first became a Christian, when people seemed to think accompanying hymns would be impossible for me. I could never understand it, but I had quite a job convincing people that I did not need to see a copy of the music before being able to play the hymns! It seemed as though their minds were quite locked into seeing a music book in front of a pianist before believing that he or she could play.

Braille music does exist, but it has to be felt to be read, of course, so would not be much help for spontaneous worship! I learned how to read Braille music when I was a child, but it is even more complicated than Braille writing, so we would not start to learn it until about the age of ten. Before that, we would learn to play pieces by rote so that we would have a selection of music to play anywhere and anytime. It gave a good foundation to memory. I have always thought that sighted children are taught to read music far too early. Music is a kind of language. When a toddler tries to talk, he is not given a book on grammar! He learns through imitation and repetition. Thus it should be for the child learning to play the piano. Imitation and repetition. If he or she were taught by rote like we were at first, they would learn to use their hands first and foremost, and have pieces 'at their fingertips'. Then, when music is eventually placed before them, I am sure they would learn to read it more easily. Most children who have piano lessons are totally tied to the music, and yet concert pianists never use written music. They memorise. It removes the inhibitions. Most people are quite lost if they don't have a music book to read from.

I admit that when I am playing for congregations I usually need to know the hymn first, but even that is not necessarily important. For instance, at Filey one year, Tim Buckley introduced the hymn 'Christ Triumphant, Ever-Reigning'. This was an entirely new hymn, comparatively recently written by Michael Baughen, who became Bishop of Chester. I had never heard it before, and neither had the organist with whom I shared the playing that morning. However, the organist could read the music so I simply followed his lead. I soon picked it up and it has been a firm favourite ever since. But even without an organist to lead, it does not seem to take me long to learn something new. Similarly I have often been asked, 'How can you play so well when you can't see the notes?' My answer to that question is always, 'How is it you can't play at all, and you can see the notes? They are always in the same places - nobody moves them about - it should be more easy for you!'

It took me some time of travelling around to various churches before people began to realise that although written music is irrelevant to me, it does not stop me from accompanying the singing. Sometimes I used to tease the people by putting up a copy of the music on the piano, and looking as though I followed it. There are still those who come to me when I do this and say, 'Can you actually read that music?' In the early days, I am sure they rather hoped I could, because then they would be convinced that I was competent to lead the congregation! When I told them I couldn't, of course, and that I was only pulling their leg, they used to seem quite disappointed! Sometimes, even nowadays, I have to sit with the congregation while a very incompetent pianist struggles to play the hymns. I suppose it is because they think I can only play limited items. It is a pity, because music makes such a big difference to the worship. There are times too, when the incompetent pianist has to be allowed to play because they would be hurt if asked to step down. They are usually described as 'faithful'.

The Scripture says, 'Well done thou good and faithful servant....'Some pianists I've heard may well be very faithful, but they are certainly not very good!

It was largely through accompanying Reg and Grace Thomlinson that my credibility as an accompanist became known. As we travelled around people would become used to the fact that I could play most things without music, and gradually they began asking me to lead the worship.

One of the first occasions when I accompanied singing other than Reg and Grace, happened when we attended a Youth For Christ meeting held in the upstairs of a building in Banbury, Oxfordshire, where the preacher was Rev. Hugh Butt from Dudley. A young woman was the regular pianist and, as usual, she was dependent upon the music.

Underneath us, downstairs, a band began to play half way through the meeting. It didn't seem too bad while we were singing, but when Hugh began to preach, the thud, thud, thud, from the drums vibrated all around and made it very hard for everyone to concentrate.

Then, at the end, in the quietness, when Hugh was about to give an appeal, the noise became really intrusive. It threatened to destroy the atmosphere completely. The young woman still sat on the piano stool, but I wished they had let me play for the singing, because I knew I could relieve the tension at this point with music. I waited until the prayer, and while all heads were bowed, I crept up to the piano.

"Excuse me," I risked, "would you mind if I took over?" The poor girl had no idea what I had in mind, but she did move away. When Hugh started the appeal, I began to play quietly. As he spoke, the music supported him and yet I played quietly enough for him to be heard clearly. It overcame the thud of the drums downstairs, but created such a good atmosphere that the appeal was saved and people were able to respond. Then I remained at the piano and played for the last hymn.

Afterwards, Hugh flung his arms around me and said, "Bless you brother! That was inspired!" It made such an uplifting difference to the meeting.

I began to be used as an accompanist for congregational singing more often after that time and each evangelist I worked with gradually accepted the fact that I would naturally play for all the singing.

It helped that they were beginning to get used to hearing such musicians as Ted Smith and Paul Mickelson who played for the Billy Graham Crusades. Their professional input obviously made such a difference that whenever possible, leaders would look for good pianists instead of simply accepting the less able regular pianists.

The next problem that began to rear its head occurred in the form of the song leader. At large gatherings like Filey, there might be three thousand in the congregation and most of the time it would be necessary to have someone standing in front conducting the singing so everyone kept together. This, in turn, meant that the organist and/or pianist would need to watch the conductor so they knew when to start and when to alter the speed of the song. This created a problem because the conductor controlled everyone except me. The conductor's waving hands could not control me. At Filey I could follow the organist who could see. 'You supply the cake and I'll ice it!' I told him. So we worked in that way. The organist, not the conductor, controlled me. Gradually, however, times began to increase when I played alone, and I would lead the congregation without the help of a song leader - or rather, the song leader would learn to sit back and let me lead!

It is all a matter of gaining the confidence of the people. I noticed especially that when I used to play for a crusade where the people had been used to singing to an organ, then they would not begin very well for me. They would have been able to come in more or less anywhere with the organ since it is not so percussive as the piano, but I found that if they did not come in with me straight away, then I could be way ahead of them in no time!

I'm afraid I dismissed from the start the idea of giving a single note as the lead to each verse of a hymn. I find that extremely amateurish, and I progressed beyond that very quickly - if I ever was at that stage!

But I would find that by the second or third night of any crusade, the people would understand my style and would soon be wholeheartedly with me, and then we could enjoy ourselves. Then, once I had gained their confidence, I could move on to the next stage - that of modulation. Being able to change from one key to another lifts the mood of the whole song.

It is quite possible to sense the mood of the people and work with them to bring out the best of the song by modulating from one key to another between verses. It is especially beneficial in songs with a last verse which contrasts to the others. For instance: the hymn, 'Man of Sorrows' has a last verse that goes: 'When he comes our glorious king........' At that point I transpose up a semi-tone and it can make a tremendous difference by lifting the spirit of the whole thing. However, it is necessary to make sure one does not overdo it. 'Familiarity breeds contempt', and if modulation happens too often, the people will tire of it and the mood will sag instead of lift.

Sometimes, given the right hymn, I can stop playing altogether and let the people take over by themselves. The third verses from 'How Great Thou Art' or 'When I Survey the Wondrous Cross' are very good examples of this. The art is getting the congregation to sing intelligently. So often they may think about what they are sing- ing in the first verse, and then perhaps switch off after that. Or with a hymn like 'And Can It Be......', they will sing loudly and confidently from the start, but forget to think about what they are singing when it gets to 'Died he for me who caused his pain, for me, who him to death pursued......' The hearty volume goes on and on, with never a thought that they are saying they pursued the lovely Lord Jesus to his death.

Once I stopped the congregation after this verse and said, 'Now I think it would be very good if we could just look at those words and see what they mean. I hope you'll forgive me for saying this, but you are a bunch of murderers.' It stopped them in their tracks! 'You can't read the words meaningfully and still sing them in the same way,' I went on. When we began again, the difference was marked. This time I was able to play much more quietly and they sang with intelligence and expression. Then when we got to 'My chains fell off, my heart was free.....' it was terrific! The atmosphere lifted and the rejoicing was tremendous!

So often the atmosphere of the place or building can make an enormous difference to the worship.

Once I played for a campaign in Enniskillen under the auspices of the Disabled Christian Fellowship, with all those taking part being disabled in some way. An even more radical difference, however, was due to the fact that it was held in the technical college and not in a church. People in Enniskillen were not used to holding meetings anywhere else but in a church, and this, unfortunately led to the meetings being mainly supported by the members of the host church. If the crusade should be held in the Presbyterian Church, then the Presbyterian denomination would support it, and they would have charge of the whole organisation including booking the speakers. Equally, this would be true of the Baptists, Methodists and Brethren, thus encouraging the denominational idea, rather than joining together in mutual worship. This is the Irish tradition, and there have been times when I have taken courage in both hands to preach about the occasion when, with Jesus in his boat, Simon Peter called to his friends to come and help bring in the large catch of fish. I dared to suggest that if one denomination called for help to another, its people would very likely be told, 'No way!' It was a very powerful message to the entrenched denominations of Ulster.

However, when we arrived in the technical college for the Disabled Christian Fellowship Campaign, we discovered that the acoustics were very poor. It really spoiled the singing, and was very disappointing. We were not at all reticent then, about changing our venue for the very last weekend, in response to a request from the college who suddenly needed to use the theatre in which we had been situated.

When we got down to the gymnasium which was to be our venue for the final few days of the campaign, we found that it was a lot narrower than the theatre, and that the acoustics were altogether different. In addition, along the walls there were alcoves where about four people could sit in each one. We realised that these would be just right for counselling people towards the end of the meeting so they wouldn't have to go right down to the front. They could just go from their particular row and sit where a counsellor could join them. It appeared so much better that we wished we had been there for the whole campaign! But when we started to sing it was clear that the acoustics were very good indeed and the singing sounded wonderful.

We finished the meeting with a magnificent rendering of 'And Can it Be.......' which prompted one of the congregation to come to us afterwards and say, "Excuse me, I've had such a blessing from that hymn in particular. I don't know if you are aware of the fact, but this gymnasium was, once upon a time, the local jail - the college is actually situated in 'Jail Square', and these alcoves around the room were once the condemned cells where prisoners spent their last days before being hanged. Even more interesting, however, is the fact that the last two people to be confined here were condemned for sheep stealing, and documentation tells us that they apparently came to know the Lord Jesus Christ as their Saviour on the night before they were hanged. It brings a whole new emphasis to the verse, 'My chains fell off...'" I knew that the atmosphere had made all the difference.

The last afternoon of that same campaign was special too. A blind lady, Carol Summerville, had brought her father to the meeting. She was part of the team, and on this afternoon she sang a song by Chris Bowater: 'Jesus Your Love Has Melted My Heart......' In the wonderful acoustics of the room, her voice just soared, and there couldn't have been a dry eye in the place - including mine. It was very special and we were all thrilled to learn that her father came to know the Lord that afternoon.

Having said all that, acoustics are not a necessary requirement for the work of the Holy Spirit to be effective. During the same campaign, the Lord worked in a wonderful way in the life of a local policeman, Victor Buchanan.

Victor's wife, Linda, had come to Christ not very long before the campaign, and she had talked him into going to one of the meetings while she remained at home to look after their children. She had been praying for him for some time, however, and others had also been praying at the prayer meetings in true Northern Ireland style: 'Lord, we want to see him sobbing his way to the cross!'

I happened to be the preacher that night, and I had quoted Matthew 18, verse 9: 'If your eye offends you, pluck it out - it is better to enter the Kingdom with one eye than have two eyes and be cast into hell.' I had no idea that Victor had been involved in some kind of bombing and had lost an eye in the process.

By the end of the meeting he was absolutely broken. He came to me weeping profusely, and I lent him a handkerchief as I counselled him. It is part of my preparation for a meeting to make sure I always have a clean handkerchief in my pocket, because if the Holy Spirit convicts a person of their sin, then they are very likely to weep. In my opinion, all counsellors should ensure that they have a clean handkerchief - one that they are prepared to give away - for just this reason.

As Victor wept he asked me, "Will it always be like this?"

"No," I assured him, "this is just the initial reaction. The tears are part of the washing process." He could not stop, however, and was in such a state that we had to arrange for him to be taken home. When Lorna opened the door, she took one look at him, threw her arms around him and laughed.

"I know exactly what's happened to you!" she said. "Praise the Lord!"

They wept together and have both been going on with the Lord ever since. It was beyond doubt that the Holy Spirit had come to Victor, and the prayers had been literally answered!

I am sure that music played a part in the whole atmosphere that led to Victor's conversion, but it was not vital to the saving process, since this particular meeting was one of those held in the theatre with the very bad acoustics. It could not be said that the Holy Spirit can only work when the surroundings are right, because he bestows his blessings where and when he wills. However, it is still right for us to create an uplifting atmosphere wherever possible.

David Shepherd, the well-known Welsh evangelist, was addressing an evangelists' conference some time ago. He said something that I shall never forget: "Brethren, as far as you are able, make sure the Good News is presented in a good atmosphere."

I believe music to be two things: it can be a breaker down of barriers, but it can also be a builder of bridges.

I understand the resentment felt by those who are brought together compulsorily to listen to me in schools or prisons. They have no choice in the same way I had no choice when I was a child at school. We were forced to attend services that had no relevance to us at all. In fact, our presence was never once even acknowledged and we hated having to go to church.

Therefore, when I go into a school, I try to let the music build a bridge. I say very little at first. I thank the head teacher and the staff for their welcome, and say 'good morning' to the children. Then I simply say , 'I want to play the piano to you first.' Sometimes the children have a favourite song. So I say, 'Let me play it for you, and you can sing it with me.' That gives a rapport straight away, but will only work in a primary school. By the time the children reach the senior school, they are not so keen on singing, so I usually play something up-beat.

I remember being in an assembly in South Glamorgan when the teacher who invited me told me afterwards, 'Before you began to play the children were quite disinterested and apathetic, with their heads down. As soon as you started paying, their heads began to rise until all their eyes were on you.'

The music breaks down the barriers and forms a bridge so that everything I say has a value. It has no value at all if I do not have the full attention of the young people.

I enjoy schools' work very much. At one particular school in Newcastle Emlyn in West Wales where several of the teachers were old friends of mine, I felt I had a very good communication with the children. After they had all gone and I was left chatting to a couple of the teachers, a boy came back into the hall.

"Excuse me, sir," he said, politely. "Could I just say 'thank you' for playing to us today?"

After he had gone, one of the teachers said, "Do you know, that boy is the biggest trouble-maker we have in the school!" Yet he was the only one to come back and say thank you.

At another school, this time in the West of Ireland, I arrived with my friend Harold Patterson, and we were walking across the playground to enter the school when a girl of about twelve years of age drew alongside and clasped my right hand.

We were soon introduced to the head teacher, who told us that we had two classes packed into one classroom. It was reminiscent of the London Tube in the rush hour. We were packed solidly. I talked to the boys and girls, and as we left, this twelve-year-old girl stuck close to me until we got to the car. We bade our farewells, and then the teacher said to the girl: "All right, Mary, you must go back to your class now." As she let go of my hand, I said to her, "Thank you, Mary, for being so caring." She went away, her face wreathed in smiles.

The teacher then said to us, "That girl is the biggest trouble-maker in school." As we drove away, we couldn't help wondering if it wouldn't solve Mary's problems to have some outlet, such as looking after a handicapped child for at least some part of the day.

I am constantly amazed at what music will do. My next development in this respect is extemporising - the art of improvising or playing music spontaneously as it comes into my head. Sometimes, if I feel the time is right, I will say to the people in a meeting, "Just sit back and maybe half close your eyes while I play to you. It will be music never heard before, and probably never heard again, so in a sense it is just for you here tonight! This gives a feeling of importance to the occasion. Then I add, "As you listen, maybe the Holy Spirit, who is here with us tonight, will bring a picture into your mind. If he does, and you want to share it with me afterwards, then please do. I'll be encouraged, but I shall also know that you have been blessed."

Some time ago in Above-Bar Church, Southampton, I did just this, and a lady came to me afterwards. She said, "A picture came to me of my sister who was so full of vitality. I could see her dancing through fields of clover and by crystal streams - she looked so vibrantly happy."

"Well, that was lovely," I said.

"Yes," she continued, "but what you couldn't realise is that my sister is, at this moment dying of cancer. I just felt that there was something prophetic about what you were playing; that this is how I would see her in the new creation."

That so blessed me. I've had other people who have shared this with me - a picture that will come simply because I believe in anointed music. I believe that music in its own right is special, but when it is anointed of God, it becomes extra-special. It seems to have that added dimension which is spiritual. Music in itself - especially extemporised music can become very ephemeral and rather temporal, but when the Spirit of God touches it, it assumes eternal qualities.

At the other end of the scale it can cause the opposite feelings, of course. Just as music can be used for good, it can be used for evil. Evil, after all, is a perversion of good. Everything was good to start with. It would be easy to exaggerate the evil side of this argument, but personally, I do feel that there is something very insidious about music like Heavy Metal - although I hesitate to use the word 'music'. Perhaps it can more accurately be described by its common nickname of 'Grunge Music'.

A pastor and evangelist friend of mine was preaching in a meeting at Haverfordwest. I was seated by the grand piano as usual. Dennis Robson was talking about heavy metal music. Suddenly he turned to me and asked, "What do you think Beethoven would have made of heavy metal, Peter?"

Quickly, I replied, "I think he would have been glad to have been deaf!"

It is the manipulation of music which worries me, and this manipulation is not only restricted to music of the media. It is possible for worship leaders to so control worship that the people are manipulated into feelings that they would not otherwise have. It is vital for any worship leader to understand that there is a point to be reached when he or she must step back and allow the people to worship without further direction. This is the art of worship-leading - knowing when to step back. The leader can direct his congregation into the paths of true worship by the way he speaks and the songs he chooses, but the moment will come - if he has done his job well - when the people are worshipping, and do not need him any more.

When I am leading the worship, I try to stand back and let the people go ahead in worship while still being available to accompany a song if and when necessary. I simply bring the people to the Lord's feet and leave them there, not interrupting them as they are speaking to him. If one interrupts one becomes a nuisance.

The art is in knowing the difference between someone who brings the people to the Lord, and someone who is a nuisance. It was John the Baptist's problem: 'He must increase and I must decrease'.

CHAPTER FOURTEEN
THE SONG - NOT THE SINGER

ACCOMPANYING SOLOISTS IS altogether different from accompanying congregational singing. It requires a particular kind of playing that gives full support to the soloist, and yet should also allow the freedom for him or her to add whatever expression they feel necessary. One soloist told me that a solo could never really be a solo unless the singer sings unaccompanied, because his or her performance is only as good as that of the accompanist. If the accompaniment is played badly, or if it supersedes the solo, then attention will be drawn to the instrument and away from the singer. It would also detract from the singer's confidence and so destroy the whole performance.

A good song should draw the attention of the audience to the song - the words in particular and not actually to the singer or the accompanist. An accompanist is just that - someone who provides a suitable backing for the singer in order to enhance the song.

My experience of accompaniment really began with my friends Reg and Grace Tomlinson who were gospel duetists and soloists in their own right in the nineteen-fifties when I was a young man. Reg and Grace taught me many gospel songs, and inspired a love for gospel singing that I've never lost. Certainly in England and Wales gospel solo singing has all but died out. It's still very much alive in Scotland and Ireland, and that must be part of the reason why I love going to those places.

I was also greatly encouraged during my holidays at Hildenborough Hall, and later Frinton, where the evangelist Tom Rees had his holiday ministry. Tom was what I would call a 'Gospel talent spotter': he would see potential and do his best to encourage it.

I shall never forget the thrill I had in playing for a hymn at Hildenborough! "Come on, Jacko, let's see what you can do," he said, christening me with the nickname which would be used often afterwards. "I want you to play for one of the praise times tonight."

I was much in awe of this well-known and rather magnetic character, and amazed that he would take the trouble to encourage me when he had other really good pianists like Gordon Brattle and Eric Alexander to play for him.

But the day came when Tom said to me, "I want you to accompany my secretary, Joyce Silcox, at the meeting tonight." Joyce had a good voice and had made several records, and I felt it a wonderful privilege to accompany her. She insisted on rehearsing, which was fine, but I soon found out that she sang very dramatically and that no matter how much rehearsing we did, she always did something entirely different in performance! I really had to be on my toes when I played for her, otherwise either one of us would be left high and dry, or I would get ahead of her - and that was a dreadful thing for an accompanist to do! Apart from Reg and Grace, Joyce was the first 'professional' I accompanied, and she stretched me to the full, thus providing me with good experience for the future.

I have accompanied many singers since that time - some of them good and some of them bad - like the two ladies who were performing in concert.... In the interval they went backstage and one who thought she was really good said to the other, "My dear, did you notice how my voice filled the hall tonight?"

"Yes," said her friend, "and did you also notice some people making room for it?"

A good soloist can create a great deal of atmosphere with the songs he or she sings and so enhance - or indeed, detract, from the worship. Some were very easy to accompany, like Eric Clarke and Peter Smith.

Once when we were in a recording session with Peter, he caused mayhem by singing 'The world will end tomorrow....' Instead of 'The world may end tomorrow...'

As soon as he had sung that first line, he might have thought the world was ending at that moment, because suddenly I threw up my hands and shouted, "False prophet! Get him out!" The rest of the team there fell about laughing as Peter wondered what he had said, and the technicians were totally bewildered.

Sometimes the emotion of the song overcame the singer - although the professional singer should learn to impart the emotion to the audience whilst staying above it himself. I remember, in particular, a father and son who came to the Shrewsbury Free Church with me on one occasion. They were Welsh, and the father was a fine singer whom I accompanied in the song, One Day I Met My Saviour. It has a very expressive refrain:

Then one day I met my Saviour,
Met him in the twilight dim,
Joy o'erwhelmed my soul and sorrow vanished.

It was very emotional, and while we were practising he got as far as this refrain and broke down. "Bach," he said, "you will go on playing even if I break down, won't you?"

"Don't worry," I assured him. "You catch me up when you've recovered!"

I remember Grace especially when she sang the song, He's Looking on You. Once when we were in Guernsey for a crusade she sang this song, and the atmosphere became so charged that there wasn't a breath stirring in the meeting and I, at least, finished with tears streaming from my eyes. Singing can be a very emotional thing.

I'm afraid opera does not do very much for me at all. I realise that it is spectacular, but I particularly dislike the sordid plots of so many operas. Someone always seems to be dying or ravished. To me, that is not what singing is all about.

Gospel singing, on the other hand, is such a wonderful medium. People sing their experience for the most part, while opera and other songs are about either fiction or legend. To me that is false in comparison with the wonderful truth of true Gospel singing. I like to encourage Gospel singers to put their feelings into words and then simply put over what the words tell them to do by their meaning.

Hymns, however, need to be kept fresh. This can be achieved by singing with intelligence and expression, but I do have another method. There are a number of well-known secular tunes that fit some hymn words very nicely. Sometimes I surprise my congregations by choosing one of these.

For instance, Blessed Assurance can be sung to the tune of Beautiful Dreamer, and In Heavenly Love Abiding will go to the old folk song tune, Annie Laurie. An old favourite, What a Friend We Have in Jesus will go very nicely to the tune of Scarlet Ribbons a song made popular one Christmas in the fifties, and There is a Fountain Filled with Blood goes to Auld Lang Syne. There are quite a number of these matches, and I deliberately do this because people tell me that 'the words came alive again'.

I sometimes use the illustration of the morning that Mr. Brown's daughter gets married. Whenever the neighbours have previously seen Mr. Brown he is in his working clothes either going to work, washing the car or doing the garden. They have never seen him in anything decent until that morning when he puts on a suit and everyone is taken by surprise - he is really quite handsome! He's the same man, but what he's wearing shows him off to advantage. Sometimes these new tunes do the same kind of thing. They have had no connection with the hymn before and it makes the people look at the words afresh.

While we are on the subject of the meaning the words, I have discovered a ministry of music that is possibly unique. It is particularly for elderly people and senior citizens. My aim is to try to get where the people are, and bring them to where I am. I draw them indirectly into what I want them to hear. If one makes a big splash, the fish will be frightened away, so I begin gently.

I take a song that the elderly folk know well - something like On the Sunny Side of the Street, and I'll say, "Do you know these words?" (I hope to develop this into having some large word charts so they can sing together.) The verse goes:

Take your coat and take your hat -
Leave your worries on the doorstep,
Just direct your feet
To the sunny side of the street.

Then I ask, "Having been on the sunny side of the street, you come home, and what's the first thing you are likely to fall over which you left on the step?"
They smile and respond with, "Our worries!"

"Absolutely!" I will say. "But have you noticed that nobody will pinch your worries with the milk.....?" I then go on to point out that the Scripture says that if we cast our burdens on the Lord, He will look after us. He doesn't say what He'll do with the burden, because it's no longer our affair. But He is willing to take it.

Another talk in similar vein comes from the song, Pack up your Troubles in your Old Kit Bag and Smile....... The old folks love to sing this song which goes back to the First World War. Then I will say, "Now, you know enough about the army to know that nobody is going to carry your kit bag for you. So what the song is saying is that you've got to carry your own troubles and grin and bear them. But the Bible says that you can cast all your anxiety on Him because He cares for you.

Then there is If you were the Only Girl in the World.... I say, "Remember what you sang? A Garden of Eden, just made for two with nothing to mar our joy......" Well, it never was made for just two. It was made to share with God. It is when we leave God out, that our joys are marred. Jesus said. My joy is in you, that your joy may be full, which suggests that there are joys, but they are never complete or full joys until we have the joy that is Jesus.

Songs like this can be taken and used to get the message home to the people because it is very much their territory. The first time I did this was with Tyne Tees Television. I did a series of epilogues for them, and developed this kind of thing quite successfully.

Yet another string to my bow in the ministry of music that God has graciously given me, is that of composing. I began learning this art as a child at school. We used to have 'Write a Tune' competitions when the teacher would ask us to write a tune by the next week. Invariably I would manage to get some sort of tune down that same day. It came quite naturally to me. I used to compose little pieces like 'The Swing Boat Song', because we had a swing boat in the playground. The swing had quite a rhythmic movement, and I tried to match its rhythm in music.

Then I wrote Merry March, and that was partly because at the beginning of the war our school was situated beside a barracks and you could hear the soldiers on parade, marching. Then as I grew older, the pieces took on a more meaningful tone. We were taught harmony and form in music - so I wrote a piece in sonata form in the style of Mozart - to illustrate that I knew about sonata form; and I also wrote pieces in the styles of Brahms, Handel and Chopin. Then, when I got to be a Gospel pianist, this ability really began to blossom.

One of the first encouragements I had in this was from Chris Pearson, who used to look after the Birmingham Male Voice Praise. In 1960 he said to me,

"Peter, I want you to be a guest pianist at the Town Hall for the Male Voice Praise Festival."

"Oh, Chris," I said, anxiously, "you'll have to send me some kind of recording of the music so I know what kind of accompaniment the choir will need......."

"No, no!" answered Chris. "I don't mean accompanying the choir - I'm asking you to come in your own right as a soloist."

"What!" I exclaimed, "play solo piano?"

"Of course," he said. "I believe that God can bless piano playing. He can anoint it to people."

I had never thought of it I those terms before, so now I embarked into another new area. I began to get together arrangements based around well-known hymns like The Love of God., bringing in some of the little choruses we learned as children such as Jesus Loves Me This I Know; then I put together a fantasy on Master the Tempest is Raging, which portrayed the rise and fall of the storm in the music, or Oh, Happy Day, in the style of Chopin. People seemed to love these 'Gospel Transcriptions', as I called them, and I went on to develop the idea.

Another encouragement came in the form of the Birmingham Youth For Christ chorus competition. I entered it and was amazed to find I won! The ability to compose was developing gradually.

When our children were born, I decided they had a to have a piece of music all their own, so Timothy Fraser, came into being first, with Christopher and Bethanie Clare following afterwards. This became my Three Piece Suite!

I have written lots of songs and choruses since that time, and although one or two were published in Word UK's first two volumes of Spirit of Praise, it is only recently that two complete volumes of my compositions have been produced. This has been published through my own company, Keynote Ministries, after many requests from all around the country for a tangible form of my work. Having started along this road, I now hope to produce more.

I have often introduced a new chorus to a congregation, who would come to me afterwards and ask for a copy of the music so they could continue to sing the song. They are always disappointed when I tell them that it has not been written down, and usually beg me to get down to publishing my music. Once, I went to an Elim Church in Erdington, Birmingham where during a chorus time some-one requested number 816. The leader looked it up and said, half turning to me, "Oh, I don't think we know this one."

"What's the first line?" I asked.

"This is where my joy is found, in Jesus...." he said.

"I think I know this one," I grinned, and started playing my own chorus which had been entered some years before in the 'Birmingham Youth for Christ' competition. I was amazed! After the meeting we checked the copyright. All it said was 'Arranged Ronan'. It had been written in the wrong key with different harmonies from mine.

But most disconcerting was that it had been submitted under the copyright of Youth For Christ. In fact, someone should have applied to me for permission to use it, and royalties should have been offered on all the Elim books sold. This, however, was not my concern. More important were the implications.

Someone involved in publication once told me, "Look, it's all very well you saying that you are not interested in royalties, but the problem is that an unscrupulous person could take one of your choruses, write down the music to it, re-arrange it a little and claim the copyright. Then you could be prosecuted for plagiarism."

"Would anyone do such a thing?" I asked.

"Oh, yes, - if it was a good enough chorus," he told me. I had never thought of it that way before, but it spurred me on to get the business of copyright sorted out. "It's not a problem of copyright," I tell some congregations, "it's a problem of copy wrong!"

I write a lot of songs nowadays, and at last it has become possible to see the best of them in print.

My wife, Margaret, is usually the first person to give an opinion on a new song. I play a new idea to her, and if she thinks it is worth developing, then I work on it a bit longer. It is always rather difficult to write in an easy style so that others can sing and play them and I feel that if the songs are worth writing, then it would be good for as many people as possible to have access to them.

I have come a long way from those days as a child when I wrote the Merry March. It's a wonderful thrill for me to know that people are praising and worshipping God in a song that he has given to me.

CHAPTER FIFTEEN

THE HOME COUNTRY

SO FAR ! HAVE TOLD you about the various areas of my life; the interesting people I have come across over the years; some of the wonderful organisations that have helped me - and many of the amusing incidents I have experienced. What I have not mentioned at any length is the most important part of my ministry - that of preaching the Word of God. So I am going to indulge myself at this point and talk about a subject that is very dear to my heart - and hopefully yours. Maybe I can throw a little light on a mysterious but exciting prospect that will joyfully affect all those who accept Jesus Christ as their Saviour and Lord...........HEAVEN.

The whole idea of Heaven is a completely foreign concept to the natural mind. There is no way that we can adequately think about it. When I was a child we had a teacher at school who had very real problems about the concept of eternity. She didn't know the Lord, of course, and used to say, 'Whenever I think of eternity, I go giddy!'

I share her misgivings in that we are trying to struggle with concepts that don't really exist down here on earth. It's like trying to tell an unborn baby about the world it is about to inhabit. Time is a kind of womb and eternity is the world into which we will be born at what we call death. It is really a metamorphosis - like the caterpillar who is very content to remain on a cabbage leaf. He knows nothing else and is quite happy and willing to struggle with trying to sustain his life. By and large he is happy with the concept he knows. But one day he looks up and sees a butterfly. Suddenly he feels insecure - disembodied. He hugs close to his cabbage leaf, not wanting to suffer the loss of that which he knows so well. He cannot conceive that the butterfly has a complete freedom and liberty. But then, inevitably, he goes into a deep sleep and wakes up when the metamorphosis is complete.

There he is, a butterfly. He soars into the air, feeling the warm currents around him, and he has a complete overall picture of things that he never had before. He previously thought entirely laterally. Now here he is, sailing away high above everything he has known. In his overall view, he sees a tiny caterpillar on a cabbage leaf and thinks, 'How I'd hate to be like that!'

So the idea of death and our entrance into Heaven, is really a birth rather than a death. It's a metamorphosis - a complete change from the physical realm to the spiritual realm. It's a change from virtual reality to ultimate reality, and it is very difficult for the virtual to comprehend the ultimate.

The problem I had in my own mind at first, was that I couldn't possibly conceive of that ultimate reality which, like the caterpillar, hemmed me into the physical reality - the here and now. Therefore that in itself could prevent me, in the long run from achieving ultimate reality. God wants us to embrace the concept of ultimate reality, otherwise we shall be confined here - and maybe even in eternity - to only virtual reality.

Of course I realise at this point, that this is Peter Jackson, the philosopher speaking, but these are the kind of things with which people are grappling, and it could be that any of our clergy are not really helping people to get to grips with what the concept of Heaven - or the hereafter, really is.

In the first place, God made Heaven and the earth, but man spoiled it and has been spoiling it ever since. Sin spoiled man. Now God is making a new creation, and eventually the Heavens and the earth will catch up with what God is doing with people. Heaven is not a confined place. It will be the Heaven and the earth that will be renewed in the new creation, and while we hare here and now part of the physical creation, yet also we are part of the new creation. One day nobody will be able to spoil it because the Heaven that is a new creation, and the new creation of Heaven will be incorruptible and undefiled so that it can never fade away.

It's the reality thing that's so important. We think that what we've got now is real. It isn't. It's a reality that is flawed and hampered. The real edge of reality is taken away by fantasies, by flawed imagination, by gratification, by money. In fact, all the things that Heaven hasn't got. Things like illness, physical and mental; a 'gone-wrong' psychology; the struggle for attainment; ambition. All these cannot be found in Heaven because it exists in ultimate reality. They are real to us because we're here. Heaven will be real to us because we're there. The comparison between the two can hardly be compared. The difference between what we know now and what we will know then, are incalculable.

Of course, God, in his Word has tried to get across to us what Heaven will be like, but even in his Word he has to use concepts with which we are familiar.

We are familiar with streets - we go out in them every day. So therefore the concept is given of a Heaven whose streets are paved with gold. When people think of gold they remember the tremendous upheaval it caused in the nineteenth century - and it might yet come to the Northern part of the British Isles since they are beginning to mine nuggets here. Gold, therefore, has been seen as the ultimate. If we could get enough gold, we would be secure for the rest of our lives. God knows the way the human mind works, so the concept of a street paved with gold makes the mind boggle! But that's the kind of concept God has to give us because that's the concept we know.

We know about rivers, so God gives us this concept that Heaven has a river. It is unpolluted - there cannot be any pollution in Heaven - so it is called the 'Crystal River'. Crystal is our ultimate in clear purity here on earth.

We know what it is to see trees, and we love to think of them - especially fruit trees because they speak of satisfaction, of shelter, of sustenance. The trees by the river in Heaven , therefore, are for the healing of the nations. The whole aspect of the unpolluted river, and the trees for health gives the wonderful concept that Heaven is the healthiest, most unpolluted place that could ever be.

We are used to buildings, so the concept of a temple was the centre of wealth because the vestments and gold were kept there. We only have to read about Solomon's temple and what he caused to be brought into it to know the wealth it contained. The concept here is wealth coupled with holiness. It is a wealth of different kind to the wealth we know down here which has to do with acquisition and rank and making sure you've got more than another person. Heaven's wealth is not that kind of wealth. It is linked to holiness with God.

Then there's the throne in the temple. In the days when this was written people were well used to thrones, royalty and power. So we have the throne which suggests authority and power, but also a centre of adoration. It is not just authority, it is obeyed authority. It represents an authority that is gladly acquiesced to, because all the people who are surrounding the throne are praising and worshipping the Lamb.

Neither is it just a symbol of imposed authority - it is invited authority.

On earth, thrones are seen as rivals. But this is not just the throne of the King of kings, it is the Throne of thrones. This authority again, like all the reality there, is ultimate - everything is ultimate - the very top.

We are all used to the concept of the sun shining. Vast sums of money are spent by the people of this country in looking for the sun. We want to get where the sun shines. It is a fact that if we could guarantee sunny summers in this country, then the holiday trade would not be suffering so much, and people would not feel the need to go abroad and spend enormous amounts just to be in the sunshine. The problem with the sunshine here is that when you get plenty of it - it's hot! Probably too hot for some people! In Heaven, the temperature is never mentioned. The reason for this is that temperature has to do with virtual reality. It can be low or high - it is variable. But in the ultimate, one doesn't need temperature. The sunshine there is not coming from the nearest star, but from the permanent Morning Star - Jesus himself. It is the light of his face that will never get hot and burn. It is soft - but even this is an earthly concept - a relativity between soft and hard.

In the ultimate you can't have differentiation, and this is where the difficulties lie - we are so used to things begin soft, hard, high, low, hot, cold, loud or quiet. There cannot be anything like that in Heaven, and if we were transported there now with our virtual reality bodies, we would not be able to cope with it. We need ultimate reality bodies that are tuned to the ultimate - and they will be one day. There again, we are using a concept - that of time, and there is no time in Heaven.

I am always amused when I play the hymn with the verse which says E'en eternity's too short to extol..... and the one which says, When we've been there ten thousand years, bright shining as the sun...... People are constantly trying to make the comparisons of time in Heaven and time does not exist there. Time is a parenthesis in eternity. We are living in a bracketed sentence.

Jesus tried to give us these concepts the best way he could. He was looking into the eyes of fishermen for the most part. There was also Matthew, an ex-tax collector for the Romans, and Simon, an insurrectionist, but the rest were mostly the uneducated poor.

They probably had the illusions and dreams of grandeur just like all of us, and they must sometimes have viewed what they called 'the mansions' of the well-off people. They were surprised when they heard Jesus say how hard it was for the rich to enter Heaven. They thought that somehow rich people had become rich because they were in favour with God. Jesus turned that on its head, however, by telling John the Baptist that the Gospel was being preached to the poor. That was the sign that proved the Messiah had really come. Jesus found it very necessary to emphasis this. He said to the men, 'Look, you've got dreams and illusions of living in great big houses because you live in poor little cottages. Well, Heaven is even better than that because I am going to prepare a place for you. And if I go and prepare a place for you, I will come again. In my Father's house are many mansions.' [11]

People have tried to translate that word 'mansion' into all sorts of things to try and make them sound.....well.....not quite so grand. But Jesus wanted to put this at the highest level possible. 'mansions' is about the best word you could use for it. 'Castles' doesn't sound the same, and neither does 'big houses'. 'Homes'? No. Mansion is exactly what it is - the ultimate in living. Jesus had to try to get this across to his disciples - and it could not be grasped any more than we can grasp Mount Everest. But God had to try through his living Word, Jesus, to present these concepts so that we would be encouraged to have faith in a God who is concerned for us, and wants to bring us into ultimate reality through his infinite love.

It is worth mentioning that the reason why Jesus promises eternal life, is because his love is infinite and if we haven't got eternal life, then sooner or later our life would run out, and love would go on loving without anything to love. If we use the word ultimate here, we would realise that there is no other life than eternal life in Jesus because it is ultimate life. This is why we have these concepts which try to get us to grasp the ungraspable. We try to conceive that inconceivable while we are here on earth.

Heaven is a place that Jesus tried to get across to us as roomy. There's plenty of room in Heaven.

When my boys were young, we were talking one day about Heaven, and Chris, the younger one of the two, said, "surely if all the people who are being saved go to Heaven, there won't be room for everybody".

Tim looked at Chris and said, "Oh, Chris, don't be so silly....." Margaret and I wondered what was coming, so I said, "Why is Chris being silly, Tim?"

"Well," he continued, "as soon as somebody gets saved, Heaven grows bigger."

That was a very interesting concept for a child. In his mind, we were not so much made for Heaven, as that Heaven was made for us, and it is a wonderful thing that there is plenty of room. If we talk about room, we are talking about the dimension we are living in now, and yet the Bible gives us measurements of the Holy City in Revelation 21 and 22, to give us the idea of there being plenty of room.

Talking of the city, Heaven, I remember travelling with a friend, Janet, to join Margaret and the boys in Guernsey, and in those days, when you got on the plane you were issued with what was called a 'landing card' which had to be filled in.

Janet was sitting beside me and she filled hers in. Then she said, "Right. Now I've got to fill in yours.' It had things like date of birth; whether the trip was business, pleasure or holiday, and then it had a very interesting line. It said, 'What city is your final destination?' - written in exactly those words.

So Janet said, "What shall I put?"

"Well, you've got to put Heaven," I said, and we laughed! And that is what she wrote because it was the only accurate answer to the question. If instead, they had asked, 'What is your final destination on this journey?', then we'd have put 'Guernsey', but the word used was 'final' so we had to be honest, didn't we?

Heaven is a place of roominess, but it is also a place which can be spoiled by nothing - absolutely nothing.

When I'm communicating the gospel to older people, I'm fond of telling the story of the lady who tried to impress her chimney sweep about his need for salvation. His response was 'Don't worry, we'll all get there in the end'.

She reminded him of the need to have his sins forgiven and to be cleansed of all unrighteousness because nothing unclean can ever go into Heaven, but he still insisted that he would be all right, and that he didn't need any formula.

Well, one day he was cleaning the particularly sooty kitchen chimney when the maid came in and said, "Madam would like to receive you in her drawing room - now".

The sweep said, "Now? I can't go in there like this."

"Well, Madam says she wants to see you now - just as you are," insisted the maid.

He was covered in soot. "Are you sure?" he asked again.

"Yes, yes. Madam says 'now'."

He knew that his employer was the kind of woman you didn't keep waiting, so he shrugged his shoulders, got up from the pile of soot in the hearth and walked off to the drawing room. As he went across the hall he left sooty prints on the carpet. Then he noticed the door of the drawing room was shut, so he knocked, transferring the soot from his knuckles to the beautiful wood panelling.

A voice said, "Come in," and he turned the creamy, white ivory doorknob - which turned black. He stood uncomfortably in the middle of the rich carpet with its beautiful deep pile, but the lady said, "Please sit down."

He noticed the beautiful braided cushions, and perched precariously on the edge of the seat. Beads of perspiration trickled down his face and neck in sooty streaks.

She handed him a cup of tea and the cup got sooty, and eventually she said, "You look very uncomfortable."

"I am, Madam," said the poor sweep. "I'm sorry that you've asked me to come into your drawing room in this state. I find it unforgivable, and I do wish you would excuse me."

"Before I do," said the determined lady, "let me just make the point that God will also excuse you from his Heaven if you come in with all your sin. In fact, it will be his mercy that excuses you, just as it is my mercy that excuses you now."

We cannot go into Heaven with our sin - or even our righteousnesses, because the Bible says that even they are like filthy rags.[12]

There must also be some kind of recognition in Heaven. I'm not sure what that means in terms of recognising each other, but there's one thing of which I am sure, and that is that we will recognise the Lord Jesus Christ. As the old Gospel song says, We shall know him by the nail prints in his hands. That recognition will be very, very special.

I have forgotten the last person that I ever saw. It might have been my mum, the nurse or the surgeon in a white coat, I don't know. I have no recollection whatsoever, but of course all things being equal, the very next person I shall see will be the Lord Jesus Christ, and until that day, written across my eyes are the words reserved for him. I know that I shall recognise him'.

A microcosm of that experience happened in my own life. In One Day I'll See You, I referred to the illness I had when I was eleven, and the emergency operation that took place. The surgeon's name was, aptly enough, Mr. James Gore, which for a surgeon is quite something! It must have been about twenty-five years after that, when I was in my thirties, I happened to mention to a customer about my wanting to meet this surgeon. I think she must have told me that her son was working at Selly Oak Hospital as a registrar, and I said, "That's where I lost my appendix, and I've often wanted to meet the surgeon so that I could thank him because he saved my life."

Mrs. Dwyer said to me, "Well I'll ask my son about that, although Mr. Gore might not still be working there."

"I shouldn't think so after twenty-five years," I said. However, word did indeed come through that he was still there, although about to retire, and the registrar arranged a meeting for us. So along I went to the hospital where I waited in anticipation for Mr. Gore to come in. It was a wonderful moment when we shook hands.

"I really do appreciate your coming to meet me," I said, "because even though you won't remember me, I just wanted to thank you for what you did all those years ago. I can tell you that from then on I have led a very full and meaningful life."

It was one of those moments you never forget - especially when he said, "In fact, I do remember you. We didn't operate on many blind children, and I remember you well. I so much appreciate meeting you." There were tears running down his cheeks, and tears were pricking the back of my eyes too.

That was a microcosm of what it will mean we see the face of Jesus. I know that he has done so very much for me, but not only will I have joy in meeting him, but he'll have joy in seeing me and presenting me - the Bible says, 'To Him who is able to keep you from falling and to present you before his glorious presence without fault and with great joy'[13] with joy - not apologies. It was the joy that was set before him[14] - the joy he anticipated, that made him think nothing of the shame of Calvary.

So you see, Heaven is recognition of the One who loved us and gave Himself for us. Heaven will be a wonderful place because there is someone wonderful waiting to receive us. If a person hasn't known the sweetness of sins forgiven and the liberty that is in Christ, Heaven will mean nothing to them. They won't even recognise the Lord Jesus and what he's done for them unless they recognise down here what He's done in them.

The songs that are given to us in Revelation are really songs about how we got to Heaven and about the means that were used to get us there. Therefore we sing, Unto Him who has loved us and freed us from sin. To Him be the glory....... and Worthy the Lamb that was slain...... Slain? What for? To redeem us to God. To bring us back to God, and if you don't know your sins have been forgiven and don't know the reality of Christ in your life, you won't be able to sing that song. These songs are sung from experience.

It reminds me of a story about a party that was attended by lots of actors, prominent people, ministers and dignitaries. Somebody thought of a bright idea. They asked one of the actors if he would recite the twenty-third psalm. He did it beautifully and the applause was long and enthusiastic.

Then there was an old minister who had been through a lot of life's experiences and counselled many people in difficult situations. A man who had learned much by experience. He too, was asked if he would recite the same psalm. When he finished, there was no applause, just a breathless silence.

Then the actor, honest and brave, said, "The difference between us is that I could say the psalm because I knew it, but this man says the psalm because he knows the Shepherd."

The songs that are sung in glory are the songs of those who have experienced what Jesus Christ has done for them. That's the beauty of Heaven. It's the culmination, the climax, of all that Jesus has done for us, and we shall be like Him. This is the new creation, part of which we are in now. We are living at present in a creation that groans and labours for that new day, when all these things shall be accomplished.

Genesis begins with the creation and the fall of man. The estrangement from God. But in the last book, Revelation, a shout goes up which fills the whole universe. It says, The dwelling of God is with men, and He will live with them. They will be His people, and God Himself will be with them and be their God[15]

That in Heaven and the whole climax of redemption. The consummation of the plan of salvation, when God is amongst us because He is our God and we are His people. Praise His wonderful name!

I hope I see you there, I really do.

FOOTNOTES

1 Acts 16: 31
2 Rev. 21; 14
3 verse 24
4 1 Thess. 5; verses 2 -3
5 1 Kings 19; 9& 10
6 Matthew 25:15
7 Isaiah 53:4
8 Proverbs 17: 22
9 Proverbs 15:23 (AV)
10 Donations can be sent to the R.N.I.B; Cromwell Road,
Bredbury, Stockport. SK6 2SG
11 John 14: 2,3
12 Isaiah 64: 6
13 Jude; verse 24
14 Hebrews 12: 2
15 Rev. 21:3